city-pick

VENICE

Oxygen Books

Published by Oxygen Books Ltd. 2010

This selection and commentary copyright © Heather Reyes 2010

Illustrations © Eduardo Reyes

Copyright Acknowledgements at the end of this volume constitute an extension of this copyright page.

All rights reserved.

No part of this publication may be reproduced, stored in a retrieval system, or transmitted in any form or by any means, without the prior permission in writing of the publisher, nor be otherwise circulated in any form of binding or cover other than that in which it is published and without a similar condition including this condition being imposed on the subsequent purchaser.

A CIP catalogue record for this book is available from the British Library.

ISBN 978–0–9559700–8–5

Typeset in Sabon by Bookcraft Limited, Stroud, Gloucestershire

Printed and bound in Great Britain by
Henry Ling Ltd, The Dorset Press, Dorchester

City of London Libraries	
BB	
CL 1187400 7	
Askews	Dec-2010
914.531 VEN	£8.99

Praise for the series

'Brilliant ... the best way to get under the skin of a city. The perfect read for travellers and book lovers of all ages'

Kate Mosse, best-selling author of *Labyrinth*

'This impressive little series'

Sunday Telegraph

'It's like having your own iPad loaded with different tomes'

The Times

'An attractive-looking list of destination-based literature anthologies ... a great range of writers'

The Independent

'There are some books that you spot and immediately curse under your breath – "Why didn't I think of that? What a great idea!" ... The editors have scoured the literature and compiled a miscellany of observations by writers, famous and insignificant, which describes the beauty, the unique character and the essence of the chosen city'

Bruce Elder, *Sydney Morning Herald*

' ... something for everyone – an ideal gift'

Travel Bookseller

'All of a sudden the traditional travel guide seems a little dull. *The Rough Guide* and *Lonely Planet* series have conditioned us to expect certain things: accommodation listings from budget to luxury, the lowdown on the best bars, restaurants and cafés, information on all the obvious sights, and the kind of prose which even makes civil war, poverty and dictatorial government seem as if they were established just to make our trip more interesting. *city-pick* offers a more soulful guide to the metropolises of the world in the company of journalists, musicians, playwrights, bloggers and novelists past and present. They are beautifully produced books and can be read from cover to cover or just dipped into. They not only fill you with an intense desire to pack bags and head away, but also to seek out the complete texts from which the extracts are taken.

Oxygen Books is restoring intellectual discovery to travelling, inviting would-be adventurers to view cities as irrepressible compositions of wisdom, wit, conflict and culture, rather than excuses to get the digital camera out and tick off another sight from the list. A very hearty bravo indeed!'

Garan Holcombe, *The Good Web Guide*

'An inviting new series of travel guides which collects some of the best writing on European cities to give a real flavour of the place ... Such an *idée formidable*, it seems amazing it hasn't been done before'

Editor's Pick, *The Bookseller*

'The perfect books for the armchair traveller as well as those of you visiting cities around the globe'

Lovereading

'A breath of fresh air ... each volume offers what it says on the tin: *perfect gems of city writing*'

Mslexia

'They are really brilliantly done – hats off!'

The Explorateur

Editor's Note

Venice, of all the world's great cities, is said to be the one most present in the popular imagination: even those who have never been there feel they already have. As the most photographed and filmed city for the purposes of advertising, our apparent familiarity with the city isn't surprising. Add to this films such as *Death in Venice*, *Don't Look Now* and *The Wings of the Dove* and the fictions they were based on, and it isn't surprising that Venice already exists in our heads. The paintings of Canaletto, the music of Vivaldi and Albinoni, and Shakespeare's *A Merchant of Venice* also create the prism through which we view the city from the moment it comes into view on our first unforgettable visit – unforgettable because Venice turns out to be much more than its familiar representation.

As always, the selection of texts represented in this anthology is just that: a selection. There are many others that could have been included (such as Peter Ackroyd's recent book on Venice, which lovers of the city will no doubt buy anyway ... and see Jeff Cotton's 'Introduction' and his excellent 'Fictional Cities' website for further reading ideas); but it is an editor's privilege to choose from personal favourites. And if yours doesn't appear here, I can only hope that being introduced to new riches will provide some compensation.

A number of the extracts in this collection are very short: they need to be read like prose-poems – little gems that capture some particular aspect of the city in the intense Venetian light. But short or long, we hope they will encourage you to look into some of the complete works from which they are taken.

Whether you already know Venice well or, as a first time visitor, still have its myriad joys, beauties and secrets to discover, we hope you enjoy exploring the city in the company of some of the best writers on the place, through their travelogues, fictions, memoirs, letters and commentaries. Some are old and some new – the old often strangely contemporary as many aspects of Venice never change, the new often rooted in the past as Venice's present exists largely by virtue of her glorious history. Set out with these writers and let their words direct your attention to more than the postcard Venice. They will help you make the most of your time in the city that remains one of the great wonders of human achievement.

Heather Reyes, 2010

Contents

Contents

Some unmissable places

"Streets full of water … "

Sights, sounds, smells … and that Venetian weather

Contents

Venetians – temporary and permanent

Contents

Art and entertainment

Parting (snap) shots

Venice by the book
by Jeff Cotton

Venice is one of the most written-about and photographed cities. 'There is notoriously nothing more to be said on the subject,' wrote Henry James in 1909, and he wasn't the first to express that opinion. He went on to qualify the statement (of course!) and then to write some more about Venice.

It's bunk to say that there's nothing new to be written, not least because with the passing of time the changing attitudes to Venice (and much more) are reflected strongly in what is written.

But talk of changing attitudes cannot mask the constants, at least as perceived by outsiders – death, decay, decline and decadence have dominated the fiction set in Venice as long as there's been fiction. As Venice has been in visible decline from its empty but picturesque eighteenth-century pomp – and some, such as Ruskin, would say the 1480s – there's been a whole lot of decay to be charted.

The mid-twentieth century was the boom time for 'serious' contemporary fiction set in Venice. Wilkie Collins's *The Haunted Hotel* had got the spooky murder thing going and Henry James's *The Aspern Papers* began the crumbling decadence strand, but it was Barry Unsworth, Daphne du Maurier and Ian McEwan, among many others, who later ran with both themes.

Less well known than Thomas Mann's *Death in Venice*, Louis Begley's *Mistler's Exit* and Robert Dessaix's *Night Letters* are also characteristic in having their central characters going to Venice to die. With the strength of this association it's not surprising that murder mysteries set in Venice load down the shelves in the English language sections of Venetian bookshops, despite the famously low levels of serious crime in the city. Donna Leon's Commissario Brunetti series is the famous force in Venice-set crime fiction, but Edward Sklepowich's winningly unfrantic Urbino Macintyre mysteries evoke warm memories of *The Thin Man*'s Nick and Norah Charles. Michael Dibdin's detective Aurelio Zen was born in Venice (the letter Z in the surname is a dead giveaway) but his only documented visit is in the novel *Dead Lagoon*, a wintry gem of Venetian writing.

Younger readers (and some older ones, too) in need of dark post-Potter thrills are made welcome in Venice too. Cornelia Funke's playful *The Thief Lord* and Mary Hoffman's moving *City of Masks* both make magic of the more sinister side of Venice's reputation for the entertainment of younger (and older) readers. And then there's Michelle Lovric's *The Undrowned Child*, the first in a series. It's a dark and warm tale set in a dank Venice where mermaids cook curries and fantastic books change lives, with its sequel, *The Mourning Emporium*, set in Venice and London at the time of Queen Victoria's funeral.

The 'literary' affinity between Venice and darkness makes it surprising that relatively little fiction has been set in the city for the period of the Second World War. The original Jewish ghetto is sited in Venice as a gift location, almost, to novelists, but only H. S. Bhabra's *Gestures* and Joseph Kanon's *Alibi* have really grasped the nettle of twentieth-century anti-Semitism and Nazism in Venice. The former like a good old-fashioned novel of intersecting lives, the latter as a gripping thriller.

Lately there's been a certain falling off of fiction set in modern-day Venice and a swing towards the historical, particularly the eighteenth-century. But this is a fashion that's far from confined to fiction set in Venice, of course.

The republic's maritime prime is well and readably dealt with in Thomas Quinn's *The Lion of St Mark* and *The Sword of Venice*, and *The Lion of Venice* by Mark Frutkin tells the tale of Marco Polo's trip East. Venice's artistic Renaissance history is oddly mostly dealt with through the exploits of modern-day art historians, who come across as somewhat unlovable individuals in David Adams Cleveland's *With a Gem-Like Flame* and Juan Manuel de Prada's *The Tempest*. The few novels actually set during the Renaissance period tend to concentrate on a strong woman's experience during repressive times – not a few nuns knocking around here.

For strong localised phenomena (and more nuns) we look to Casanova and Vivaldi, and the eighteenth-century Venice that they share. The very readable volumes of Casanova's own *History of My Life* have fed some equally enjoyable novels, including Michelle Lovric's *Carnevale*, and some racy biographies, the most recent being by Ian Kelly. Andrea di Robilant's *A Venetian Affair* gives us more love and intrigue during this period.

But Casanova's world of debauchery and masked deception has recently given way to fictional accounts of the life of Antonio Vivaldi. You'll need both hands to count the number of late-noughties novels dealing with speculation regarding what one might politely call the composer's domestic arrangements. Not much is actually known about his life, and so the scope to invent, particularly with regard to his relationship with his young protégés at the Pietà (and one Anna Giro in particular) is considerable. The best of these novels have been *The Four Seasons* by Laurel Corona, which features Vivaldi as something of a secondary, though charismatic, character whilst exploring the lives of two sisters left at the Pietà, and *Hidden Harmonies: the Secret Life of Antonio Vivaldi* by André Romijn, which concentrates on the composer and makes some wild guesses at the nature of his relationship with

Anna Giro, but also deals deeply and revels in the music. And then spring 2011 sees the much-anticipated publication of the English translation of Tiziano Scarpa's *Stabat Mater* – an actual Venetian's take on Vivaldi, seen from the point of view of one of his students.

Sharing Casanova's status as one of the essential primary sources is Marin Sanudo, whose diaries, recently collected plushly by Patricia H. Labalme and Laura Sanguinetti White in a book called *Venice, Città Excelentissima*, show us a Renaissance Venice rife with political intrigue. Also during this period Englishman Thomas Coryate provides some much less dry commentary, from a visitor's perspective. In the interests of research, he samples and describes Venetian food and prostitutes with equal gusto and wonderment.

Ruskin's *Stones of Venice* dominates the section of the library devoted to attempts to define and distil Venice – it's a big book and, some say, better read about than read. More recent attempts have tended to be less substantial and more journalistic. Judith Martin's *No Vulgar Hotel* pretty much nails the signs and symptoms of Venice-love, whilst Bidisha's *Venetian Masters* is less ingratiating. Amongst the quirkier and more creative summaries Italo Calvino's *Invisible Cities* is the famous standout, although there have been more accessible attempts at such poetic distillation, like *The Other Venice* by Predrag Matvejević and Tiziano Scarpa's *Venice is a Fish*. But the best-known of these attempts at definition is Jan Morris's *Venice*. Along with the Ruskin, guidebooks by Lorenzetti and Links, and John Julius Norwich's *History*, it forms the foundation of the Venetian bookshelf. Less well-known is William Dean Howells' *Venetian Life* – the American author's diplomatic posting to Venice dropped him into an old world wholly new to him and the resulting book is a gem of urbane humour set during the Austrian occupation and hence well into the years of dark decline.

Everyone has their own bookshelf, of course, and their own idea of Venice. Decay, canals, cats, *gelati* ... we all start with the same basic ingredients, but the extracts in this book are the spices that will make our experience of the city – as tourists or simply as armchair travellers – that much more flavoursome.

JEFF COTTON writes about novels set in Venice (and about films, cats, cakes, churches and scaffolding) on his websites fictionalcities.com and churchesofvenice.com.

Arrival – by sea, land and air

Many travellers will tell you that the best way to arrive in Venice is by sea. They may be right, but each kind of arrival – whether by ship, train, car or plane – has its own special pleasures. First we sail in with travel writer Jan Morris, whose Venice *is one of the best-known books on the city.*

At 45°14'N., 12°18'E., the navigator, sailing up the Adriatic coast of Italy, discovers an opening in the long low line of the shore: and turning westward, with the race of the tide, he enters a lagoon. Instantly the boisterous sting of the sea is lost. The water around him is shallow but opaque, the atmosphere curiously translucent, the colours pallid, and over the whole wide bowl of mud-bank and water there hangs a suggestion of melancholy. It is like an albino lagoon.

It is encircled with illusory reflections, like mirages in the desert – wavering trees and blurred hillocks, ships without hulls, imaginary marshes: and among these hallucinations the water reclines in a kind of trance. Along the eastern reef strings of straggling fishing villages lie empty and unkempt. Away in the wastes there stand the sails of fishing boats, orange, yellow and magenta, with cabalistic signs or heraldic symbols, a rampant red horse, an all-seeing eye. The shallows are littered with intricate shambling palisades of sticks and basket-work, and among them solitary men, knee-deep in sludge and water, prod in the mud for shellfish. A motor boat chugs by with a stench of fish or oil. A woman on the shore shouts to a friend, and her voice eddies away strangely, muffled and distorted across the flats.

Silent islands lie all about, lapped in marsh and mud-bank. Here is a glowering octagonal fort, here a gaunt abandoned lighthouse. A mesh of nets patterns the walls of a fishermen's islet, and a restless covey of boats nuzzles its water-gate. From the ramparts of an island barracks a listless soldier with his cap over his eyes waves half-heartedly out of his sentry-box. Two savage dogs bark and rage from a broken villa. There is a flicker of lizards on a wall. Sometimes a country smell steals across the water, of cows or hay or fertilizer: and sometimes there flutters in the wake of the boat, not an albatross, but a butterfly.

Presently this desolate place quickens, and smart white villas appear upon the reef. The hump of a great hotel protrudes above the trees, gay parasols ornament a café. A trim passenger steamer flurries southwards, loaded deep. A fishing flotilla streams workmanlike towards the open sea. To the west, beneath a smudge of mountains, there is a thin silver gleam of oil drums, and a suggestion of smoke. A yellow barge, piled high with pop bottles, springs from a landing-stage like a cheerful dove from an ark. A white yacht sidles indolently by. Three small boys have grounded their boat on a sand-bank, and are throwing slobbery mud at each other. There is a flash of oxy-acetylene from a dark shed, and a barge stands on stilts outside a boat yard. A hooter sounds; a bell booms nobly; a big white sea-bird settles heavily upon a post; and thus the navigator, rounding a promontory, sees before him a city.

It is very old, and very grand, and bent-backed. Its towers survey the lagoon in crotchety splendour, some leaning one way, some another. Its skyline is elaborate with campaniles, domes, pinnacles, cranes, riggings, television aerials, crenellations, eccentric chimneys and a big red grain elevator. There are glimpses of flags and fretted rooftops, marble pillars, cavernous canals. An incessant bustle of boats passes before the quays of the place; a great white liner slips towards its port; a multitude of tottering palaces, brooding and monstrous, presses towards its water-front like so many invalid aristocrats jostling for fresh air. It is a gnarled but gorgeous city: and as the boat approaches through the last church-crowned islands, and a jet fighter screams splendidly out of the sun, so the whole scene seems to shimmer – with pinkness, with age, with self-satisfaction, with sadness, with delight.

The navigator stows away his charts and puts on a gay straw hat: for he has reached that paragon among landfalls, Venice.

Jan Morris, *Venice* (1960)

✳ ✳ ✳

Kay MacCauley and Jeanette Winterson evoke the age-old magic of seeing Venice for the first time.

Merchants sailing from the Adriatic, through the sea-gate of the Lido, would see rising into view before them a vast glittering expanse of domes, cupolas and towers, jewel-greens, purples and golds, with outlines that shimmered and shifted against the vapour that rose up from the Lagoon. Their astonishment would grow on drawing into the quay of San Marco and finding it not mirage but real.

Kay MacCauley, *The Man Who Was Loved* (2006)

✳ ✳ ✳

Arriving at Venice by sea, as one must, is like seeing an invented city rise up and quiver in the air. It is a trick of the early light to make the buildings shimmer so that they seem never still. It is not built on any lines I can fathom but rather seems to have pushed itself out, impudently, here and there. To have swelled like yeast in a shape of its own. There are no preliminaries, no docks for the smaller craft, your boat anchors in the lagoon and in a moment with no more ado you are in St Mark's Square.

Jeanette Winterson, *The Passion* (1987)

✻ ✻ ✻

Thomas Mann's novel, Death in Venice, *describes arrival by water in more detail but with an equal sense of wonder, excitement and anticipation.*

The flat coast showed on the right, the sea was soon populous with fishing-boats. The Lido appeared and was left behind as the ship glided at half speed through the narrow harbour of the same name, coming to a full stop on the lagoon in sight of garish, badly built houses. Here it waited for the boat bringing the sanitary inspector. [...]

... the machinery began to thud again, and the ship took up its passage through the Canal di San Marco which had been interrupted so near the goal.

He saw it once more, that landing-place that takes the breath away, that amazing group of incredible structures the Republic set up to meet the awe-struck eye of the approaching seafarer: the airy splendour of the palace and Bridge of Sighs, the columns of lion and saint on the shore, the glory of the projecting flank of the fairy temple, the vista of gateway and clock. Looking, he thought that to come to Venice by the station is like entering a palace by the back door. No one should approach save by the high seas, as he was doing now, this most improbable of cities.

The engines stopped. Gondolas pressed alongside, the landing-stairs were let down, customs officials came on board and did their office, people began to go ashore. Aschenbach ordered a gondola. He meant to take up his abode by the sea and needed to be conveyed with his luggage to the landing-stage of the little steamers that ply between the city and the Lido. [...]

Is there anyone but must repress a secret thrill, on arriving in Venice for the first time – or returning thither after long absence – and stepping into a Venetian gondola? That singular conveyance, come down unchanged from ballad times, black as nothing else on earth except a coffin – what pictures it calls up of lawless, silent adventures in the plashing night; or even more, what visions of death itself, the bier and solemn rites and last soundless voyage! And has anyone remarked that the seat in such a bark, the arm-chair lacquered in coffin-black, and dully upholstered, is the softest, most luxurious, most relaxing seat in the world? Aschenbach real-ised it when he had let himself down at the gondolier's feet, oppo-site his luggage, which lay neatly composed on the vessel's beak. The rowers still gestured fiercely; he heard their harsh, incoherent tones. But the strange stillness of the water-city seemed to take up their voices gently, to disembody and scatter them over the sea. It was warm here in the harbour. The lukewarm air of the sirocco breathed upon him, he leaned back among his cushions and gave himself to the yielding element, closing his eyes for very pleasure in an indolence as unaccustomed as sweet. 'The trip will be short,' he thought, and wished it might last forever.

Thomas Mann, *Death in Venice* (1912)
translated by H. T. Lowe-Porter

*   *   *

In Caryl Phillips' The Nature of Blood, *a new arrival finds himself unprepared for the grandeur and glory of the city.*

I arrived in the spring and was immediately enchanted by this city-state. I approached by water and found myself propelled by the swift tides across the lonely empty spaces of the forbid-ding lagoon. I stepped out on deck and observed the grey choppy seas, the high arch of the sky, and then looked across the distant low horizons to the monasteries, forts and fishing villages of the surrounding islands. Above me, the sails and flags snapped in the damp Venetian wind, and then, to our side, I spied a boatman hurrying back to the city ahead of the oncoming storm, with swallows flying low and skimming the water to either side of his unsteady vessel. As we neared the city, the air became warm and moist, and its smell somewhat like the breath of an animal. Then the water began to lap less vigorously, and bells began to sound, and I suddenly found myself to be surrounded by the raised voices of gondoliers; and then, as though following strange music, I discovered myself being sucked into the heart of Venice. What ingenuity! Nothing in my native country had prepared me for the splendour of the canals, but it was not only these waterways which seized my attention. The magnificence of the buildings that lined the canals overwhelmed my senses, and upon the grandest of these buildings, proud images of the Venetian lion were carved in wood, chiselled in stone, or wrought in iron. I could barely tear my eyes from the genius of these palaces, for they suggested to me the true extent of my journey into this fabled city. I had moved from the edge of the world to the centre. From the dark margins to a place where even the weakest rays of the evening sun were caught and thrown back in a blaze of glory.

Caryl Phillips, *The Nature of Blood* (1997)

✳ ✳ ✳

For great German writer Johann Wolfgang von Goethe, part of the pleasure of arriving in Venice for the first time is turning a familiar word into reality.

It was written, then, on my page in the Book of Fate that at five in the afternoon of the twenty-eighth day of September in the year 1786, I should see Venice for the first time as I entered this beautiful island-city, this beaver-republic. So now, thank God,

Venice is no longer a mere word to me, an empty name, a state of mind which has so often alarmed me who am the mortal enemy of mere words.

When the first gondola came alongside our boat – this they do to bring passengers who are in a hurry to Venice more quickly – I remembered from early childhood a toy to which I had not given a thought for perhaps twenty years. My father had brought back from his journey to Italy a beautiful model of a gondola; he was very fond of it and, as a special treat, he sometimes allowed me to play with it. When the gondolas appeared their shining steel-sheeted prows and black cages greeted me like old friends.

Johann Wolfgang von Goethe, *Italian Journey [1786–1788]*
translated by W. H. Auden and Elizabeth Mayer

* * *

For Venetian Paolo Barbaro, it doesn't matter how you arrive: as soon as you board the vaporetto, something odd happens to time and perception …

But it's not just the atmosphere and the weather that change as soon as we're on the lagoon. Clock time changes, too, every single time. We're forced to set our watches and selves to an entirely different rhythm.

You step down from the train. You get out of the car. You take a few paces, climb onto the boat, and it changes. The tick-tock of your watch is different. You can see and feel it right away: the velocity of the vaporetto is more or less a twentieth of the velocity of your car. You can feel it on your skin as soon as you set foot on the boat – that you're not so much travelling across the water as uneasily decelerating, coming to a slow halt. Motion and the measure of motion, the sense and rhythm of time are completely different now. Perhaps time expands; for sure it slows down. Will we live longer this way?

With everything slowed down, our glance becomes sharper and more attentive. We're less insensible, and things become more visible; at last we can see, observe, and feel. Walls and houses slide by. We glimpse someone on the riva and are struck with a desire to reach out and communicate. Little by little the miracle unfurls within us: we see as we feel and feel as we see. Even the sky changes. To be more exact: *this is the sky*.

It's pale blue, pearled and gilded, multiplied by the water it hovers above, according to the day and the hour. And it's azure fog, white wind of the bora, mist swirling into the soul – it depends on us, on what we let in.

Paolo Barbaro, *Venice Revealed* (1997)
translated by Tami Calliope

✳ ✳ ✳

The Venice-loving American novelist Henry James briefly recalls arriving by train.

I came into Venice, just as I had done before, towards the end of a summer's day, when the shadows begin to lengthen and the light to glow, and found that the attendant sensations bore repetition remarkably well. There was the same last intolerable delay at Mestre, just before your first glimpse of the lagoon confirms the already distinct sea-smell which has added speed to the precursive flight of your imagination; then the liquid level, edged afar off by its band of undiscriminated domes and spires, soon distinguished and proclaimed, however, as excited and contentious heads multiply at the windows of the train; then your long rumble on the immense white railway-bridge, which, in spite of the invidious contrast drawn, and very properly, by Mr. Ruskin between the old and the new approach, does truly, in a manner, shine across the green lap of the lagoon like a mighty causeway of marble; then the plunge into the station, which would be exactly similar to every other plunge save for one little fact – that the keynote of the great medley of voices borne back from the exit is not "Cab, sir!" but "Barca, signore!"

Henry James, *Italian Hours* (1909)

* * *

Even if the best way to approach Venice for the first time is by sea, approaching by train also has its pleasures.

Everyone should enter Venice from the sea at least once, but for me, now that her Empire has gone and the great argosies which sailed from her sheltered waters have been replaced by fleets of gondolas depending on the petty cash of tourism, the sea approaches seem strangely empty, as though the dazzling image rising from the sea, so beloved by film-makers, were only in fact a glittering rococo picture frame from which the design for which it was created has been ripped, leaving it pretty but useless, a home without inhabitants. From the mainland, however the approach was, and is quite different. [...]

My first awareness of the approach was the fading of the olive groves, and sudden tangy whiffs of the sea. Then suddenly we were in a small industrial town (it has grown greatly since) and a railway station called Venezia Mestre. [...]

... and suddenly the train seemed to be on water, the thin spit of land between the rails seemed to disappear from view, and we were in the back waters of Venice, calm and blue, reflecting a light I fell in love with then and there; the first time, I believe, I fell in love with anything in all my life. It is only now that I know enough to be able to warn young men to be wary of anything they do, or say, or most of all feel, when they fall into the company of that most unlikely thing to the English mind, an interesting woman.

The waters were studded with little fishing boats piled high with nets, some of them moored to rickety poles, and in the water first we caught sight of the workaday face of Venice, the barely adorned brick she presents to what was once her land-bound empire, a plain and practical face, reflective of the mercenary mind which paid for all the decorations she faces to the sea. Then steam and smoke and smuts flew backward, and we were there.

H. S. Bhabra, *Gestures* (1986)

✳ ✳ ✳

In An Equal Music, *contemporary British novelist Vikram Seth has his characters arrive by the afternoon train.*

I go back to the compartment. Julia is awake. We do not speak much, but point out of the window from time to time at things we want to share. [...]

Soon we are in the Veneto: walls of terracotta and ochre, a red-roofed town in the shadow of a hulking mountain; elderberries along the track; gardens of irises and pink roses; the junkyards and sidings of Mestre.

As we move swiftly along the causeway across the grey-green water of the lagoon, the beautiful city draws itself into our eyes: towers, domes, façades. If a few years late, we are here at last. The two of us stand in the corridor with our luggage and look out over the water. [...]

Four-thirty on a weekday afternoon is no magical time. But I stand on the steps of the station, almost leaning against Julia, and succumb to the smell and the sound of Venice, and the dizzying sight.

The terminal has disgorged us with hundreds of others. It is not the high tourist season, but we are plentiful enough, and I gape, as it is right I should, for all of it is undisappointingly beautiful.

"So this, then, is the Grand Canal."

"This, then, is it," says Julia, with a smile.

15

"Should we have come by sea?"

"By sea?"

"By sea at sunset?"

"No."

"No?"

"No."

I grow quiet. We are sitting at the front of the vaporetto as it chugs along in its soft pragmatic way, bumping against its landing stages, taking on and setting off passengers. All around is a lively, thrumming, car-less, unhectic sound.

A breeze eases the heat of the day. A gull flies down to the murky turquoise water, quick with flecks of light.

Solidly, fantastically, the palaces and churches that wall the canal pass by on either side. My eyes take in a casino, a sign to the Ghetto, a lovely garden with wisteria entwined over a trellis. A small working boat with two young men in orange shirts, putters past the vaporetto. An elegant older woman, with fat pearls and a brooch, gets on at Ca' d'Oro, followed by a woman pushing a pram containing her shopping. The green scum at the edge of the water stretches up the stone steps, the striped mooring-poles.

"What would Venice do without geraniums?" says Julia, looking upwards. [...]

The stone bridge at the Rialto, the wooden bridge at the Accademia, the great grey dome of the Salute, the columns and bell-tower of San Marco, the pink-and-white confection of the Doge's palace pass over us or by us one after the other; and all so luxuriously, so predictably, so languidly, so swiftly, so astonishingly that there is something about it that is disturbing, almost gluttonous. It is a relief to be in the open basin of the lagoon, unhemmed by gorgeousness.

Vikram Seth, *An Equal Music* (1999)

❋ ❋ ❋

For the narrator of Brideshead Revisited, *however, it's a
relief to leave the hot, crowded, smelly train – the slow
one from Milan – and step into a waiting gondola …*

The sun mounted high and the country glowed with heat; the
carriage filled with peasants, ebbing and flowing at each station,
the smell of garlic was overwhelming in the hot carriage. At
last in the evening we arrived at Venice.

A sombre figure was there to meet us. 'Papa's valet, Plender.'

'I met the express,' said Plender. 'His Lordship thought you
must have looked up the train wrong. This seemed only to
come from Milan.'

'We travelled third.'

Plender tittered politely. 'I have the gondola here. I shall
follow with the luggage in the *vaporetto*. His Lordship had
gone to the Lido. He was not sure he would be home before
you – that was when we expected you on the Express. He
should be there by now.'

He led us to the waiting boat. The gondoliers wore green
and white livery and silver plaques on their chests; they smiled
and bowed.

'*Palazzo. Pronto.*' […]

The palace was a little less than it sounded, a narrow
Palladian façade, mossy steps, a dark archway of rusticated
stone. One boatman leapt ashore, made fast to the post, rang
the bell; the other stood on the prow keeping the craft in to the
steps. The doors opened; a man in rather raffish summer livery
of striped linen led us up the stairs from the shadow into light;
the *piano nobile* was in full sunshine, ablaze with frescoes of
the school of Tintoretto.

Our rooms were on the floor above, reached by a precipi-
tous marble staircase; they were shuttered against the afternoon sun; the butler threw them open and we looked out on
the Grand Canal; the beds had mosquito nets.

'*Mostica* not now.'

There was a little bulbous press in each room, a misty, gilt-framed mirror, and no other furniture. The floor was of bare marble slabs.

'A bit bleak?' asked Sebastian.

'Bleak? Look at that.' I led him again to the window and the incomparable pageant below and about us.

'No, you couldn't call it bleak.'

Evelyn Waugh, Brideshead Revisited (1945)

✳ ✳ ✳

Approaching Venice by road may not be the most romantic way to arrive, but at least you get to see what is probably the most famous car park in the world. And it doesn't take long to get from there to the beauty at the heart of the city. In Brigid Brophy's novel, The King of a Rainy Country, *a film crew arrives by road.*

In the afternoon Carlo chugged along without hurry. We had time to read each of the advertisement placards propped up along the verge of the road like the sandwich boards carried by card kings. We turned off and crawled along the dusty road beside the sun-dappled Brenta; in the late afternoon we reached the sea, saw the gasworks and shipyards lying under smoke to our right, and at last found ourselves on the long bridge to Venice. Undeviating, the road stretched ahead like an airstrip. Militaristically straight, the railway went side by side with it. We cut our way over flat, razor-blade blue sea, that seemed to be nearly on a level with the road. The sun behind us lit up the rear window of the coach. Occasionally, on the surface of the water, it touched off a light on one of the faces of a ripple.

Mrs. Luther said, "Are we near Venice? We're behind schedule."

"Very nearly there."

"We got to get there soon."

At last we came to land. We drove past the notice pointing, in English, to the ferry. Carlo carried us on, into the Piazzale Roma. The yellowish tiered garage rose on our right. Carlo drove carefully between the local buses and their concrete islands, and drew up at the far end where patches of oil glistened on the road, under the shade of trees hanging over from the small public garden.

We got out; I gave Mrs. Luther directions; we engaged porters.

Carlo climbed down from the driving seat. "Allora."

"Allora."

We shook hands with him.

"Arivederci."

"Arivederci."

The porters went ahead, the luggage slung round them. We led the party down the short path through the garden. One side was shaded; peasant women in black were sitting on the low, artificially rural wall. The other side was in the sun, and ants swarmed.

We emerged on to the bright, broad quay. The church opposite, its stone shimmering in the sum, seemed to rock gently on the far side of the canal.

"Gondola, signori, gondola, gondola."

We calculated, and engaged ten. We grouped the party at the steps. The gondolas queued, nuzzling each other. We tried to make up parties to offend no one's friendships, no one's snobberies. We filled one boat, Neal and the old man with the boat-hook handing the passengers in; we piled the suit-cases, up-ended at front and back; the boat pushed off, the next one moved up. Each woman, as she stood with one foot on land and lowered the other over the edge until it touched the bottom of the boat and felt it softly give way, made a tiny shriek.

The men said: "You're riding too low in the water." "What payload do you carry?" "Does a gondola ever sink?" Tad tried on a gondolier's hat.

We saw them off.

A gondolier approached us. We shook our heads. "We can beat them to it if we go by vaporetto," said Neal. "If we get a direct one." We queued at the kiosk, bought tickets for ourselves and our luggage, and passed on to the rocking landing-stage. The boat came: the platform jarred mildly. The official rattled open the brass rail, jumped on to the stage, secured the rope; he unchained our exit and we stepped on to the boat. We piled our luggage on the steps beside the helmsman's cabin, and moved forward, deep into the crowd, deep into the prow. "It's fantastically efficient, isn't it?" said Neale.

The sides of the boat curved high round us. When we cut another boat's wake we got wet.

We sailed up, between deep orange and rose-pink; between Venetian gothic and Venetian baroque. The sun divided the surface of the water first into strips and patches, then into transparent tesseræ.

We stared, not minding that the brightness wounded our eyes.

Brigid Brophy, *The King of a Rainy Country* (1956)

✳ ✳ ✳

Like the characters in Brigid Brophy's novel, writer Bidisha, taking the airport bus, also gets her first taste of Venice – heat and traffic fumes – at the Piazzale Roma.

On the bus from Treviso Airport to Venice I can see square, shuttered, chalkily tinted villas behind long paths and spiked gates. Everything's dry and sunny. At a crossing I spot a young man on a bicycle, a brown-haired angel beamed down from Planet Chic: dark brown slim trousers, a slightly lighter brown fitted jacket, an olive green shirt buttoned up to the top, charcoal grey waistcoat, leather satchel. Slim, lovely face and abundant dark, wavy hair, straight out of a cigar advert. I'm visiting

Venice for the first time, staying at a palazzo owned by the family of my best friend, Stefania.

I arrive at the bus station at Piazzale Roma, get off and immediately feel the May heat. The sun's fat in the sky and dripping like syrup. I don't log much except the grimy smell of exhaust fumes, the number of buses and the sun shining off them. This is the western corner of Venice, attached to the big spiral car park at Tronchetto, the motorway and the single route to the mainland. I make for the green-topped shelter where I'm meant to meet Stefania's childhood friend Ginevra – Stefania's at a meeting in Rome today. An older couple in their sixties, turtle-like, in glowing chocolate brown furs (never let the climate stop you wearing your money), kid gloves and dark shades, pointedly don't get out of my way when I try to stagger past with my huge sausage-shaped sports bag. They stand like the king and queen in a deck of cards, holding hands across the pathway.

Eventually Ginevra and I spot each other. She comes forward and asks me mildly how the journey was and if I want anything. Ginevra's very pretty, big-handed and tall and slender, caramel-coloured long hair with a fringe, tortoiseshell-framed glasses and pale, dry skin. Marvel at the elegance: her clothes match her colouring perfectly, fawn cord trousers, caramel fitted leather jacket, green silk scarf. I give Ginevra my rucksack and take the sausage bag myself. We're due to drop everything off at Stefania's apartment in Cannarego, in the north of the city.

'Here it is not so beautiful,' says Ginevra regretfully, in English, in her light, cultured, descending voice.

'It's very beautiful,' I say shortly. 'The light. But I know that's a cliché.'

'But I do not see you looking so astonished … '

'No, but I am. I can't believe I'm here, at last.'

Bidisha, *Venetian Masters* (2008)

✳ ✳ ✳

Finally, we fly in with Paolo Barbaro, returning to his native city in winter. The perspective from the sky shows some negative aspects of the industrial areas just beyond the jewel of Venice itself, but don't the shifting colours and shapes, the many Venices seen from the sky, still have the power to enchant?

"We are approaching our landing in Venice," they repeat, "*Venezia, Venise, Venice, Venedig.*" In fact, what immediately appears, instead of Venice, is Marghera. Oil tanks, hangars, cranes, loading docks, power plants.

Seen from above, the powerful industrial zone stretches endlessly along the fragile and imperiled water. Concentrated, spreading, grandiose, a vision of hell rises up from the slender strand where earth meets lagoon, a hell with its own eager and sinister beauty.

I recognise the enormous factory gliding beneath the descending plane, and follow the shadows of wings over its warehouses and towers. For years I have worked, all over the world, in great industrial centres like this one: Marghera has been their model. How much human labour, effort, money, thought. And now worries, anger, and problems: so many more than we had ever thought possible – in the waters, on the earth, among peoples. The shadow of the plane passes swiftly away, as do the factory, the power plants, the plane itself. As do the years.

I glimpse an oil tanker in the lagoon – slow, almost motionless – arriving from the Canale dei Petroli. It ploughs stolidly into red and yellow waters spitting out effluents-discharges-arabesques, a profound and seasoned pollution. And who will ever wash it clean now? Soon the tanker will moor itself to one of those white wharves. "Like a toy!" they shout in the airplane, laughing. Maybe, but for me, remembering what this expanse of earth-water-world was like only a few years ago, it's no toy; it's no joke. Instead, it's a deadly trap between shoals and sandbars, a few inches of water – I can see it clearly from here. And it's all so close to the waiting houses, the tiny gardens – to Marghera, to Venice. And yet it all continues, as if the years weren't going by: the protests against the oil in the lagoon, the agonising over red pollution or yellow waste, visible or invisible, are words in the wind, useless.

Early evening and we're already on the runway, or maybe still over the water; but Venice is there, in the fog on the other side of the plane. I glimpse the puffs of distant cupolas – or clouds, perhaps – and the spires of bell towers like the masts of ships: the other part of the world. In the pale winter light, more moon than sun, we begin to invent Venice.

And yet today, as the family comes back home to stay, we're in luck: there's traffic between sky and earth, so the plane is making a slow descent. "A minute or so more," they repeatedly assure us, "a moment or so more to wait." We wheel in the air, over islands, coasts, and tracts of ocean. They are giving us a small gift of time – right here, in the airplane, one of the great time-destroyers. But how can I get this across to the kids, who are ever more impatient? They want to "arrive".

Thomas Mann was right, Venice should be approached from the sea. But now there's the sky; millions of beings drop down every day from the clouds. Today we're arriving at sunset, sliding through tremendous rents of light over the waters, from one horizon to the other. The kids crowd together on the other side of the airplane, piled up on top of the Japanese, the Brazilians, the Americans …

But here it is at last, appearing suddenly and in its entirety: the long, rose-coloured island in the perfect form of a fish, immersed and emerging, born in this moment for us. "What is it?" asks a little boy, sprouting up out of the front seats, seeing and not seeing.

A city I don't know, I should tell him. I don't know what to call it, since "Venice", by now, is a thing that gleams on the backs of a million glossy postcards.

"What is it?" he insists. "What fish is it?"

"It's the Venice-Fish," I say. "Don't you see it?" He seems happy enough.

I look down on it again myself: Venice, mysteriously interrogatory and enchanted, tranquil and troubled. Pathetic, motionless, delicate – sailing, maybe. But who put it together, this living event at once miniscule and enormous, this impeccable shape built of infinite, shapeless scales? Is it a miracle of human life? A random act of nature?

Island upon island, dusky molecules, houses great and small, compact, solid, dreaming, waiting; rare the empty spaces, the piazzas, the gardens. Canals, banks, mirrors and more mirrors: clear or opaque, reflections of reflections, dazzling. And the great blue-green expanse that reassembles, recomposes everything. There is a moment of silence in the airplane, our fraction of eternity. Japanese, Brazilians, Venetians ... who are we, really, in here, but a group of individuals, big and little, young and old, spying on the flower of stone in the sea from on high?

An instant later, it's there, in the centre of the island: a black hole, a square piazza – Piazza San Marco, hollowed out from the heaped-up cluster of houses, brushed ever so lightly by the lagoon, which now has begun to rise and fall like a plane in the gusts of wind, in the heart of the Venice-Fish. The nearest surrounding islands tilt and press toward the centre for safety; the farthest begin to cast off their moorings, to depart even as they arrive. The plane drops and wheels, the lagoon changes colour with every turn: green-lagoon among the curls of white foam, green-yellow-blue, green-rose lagoon. The sunset intensifies, streaking the sky with violet and orange.

We've arrived at low tide, that's easy to see now. How many possible Fish, how many versions of Venice, are under us here? They are being born and reborn in the water and mud, ready to replace ours, now that it's starting to vanish ... appearing perhaps one time only in the history of the world.

At almost the same moment – on the islands, in the water, on each small scale – the streetlamps come on, doubling the reflections, the season, the hour, the evening, the strangeness of this beauty. In reality, we realise, thinking back for a moment to the metropoli we've lived in, Venice is small, Venice is very little. It's tiny and fragile, this flower of stone. In contrast the lagoon is so big; the sea is so big; and the cities we've loved in our life disappear, are destroyed.

And here we are on the runway – it's really earth, a sudden strip of earth. But we don't want to land, to return to the planet; miracles are brief, especially celestial ones. Set foot in Venice? I still hesitate to say it, even: Venice, *Venezia*. I only know that I feel doubly alive, between the rediscovered earth and the waiting water. And so do they, the little band that's following me.

"Have we arrived?"

"Yes, we've arrived."

Paolo Barbaro, *Venice Revealed* (1997)
translated by Tami Calliope

For the love of Venice

It's almost impossible not to fall in love with Venice. But before we start on the litany of praises from all kinds of people of different times and origins, let's look at an exception and get the 'bad news' out of the way first. When Edward Lear (best known for his 'nonsense poems') visited Venice in the mid-nineteenth century, this was his response:

Now, as you will ask me my impressions of Venice, I may as well shock you a good thumping shock at once by saying I don't care a bit for it and never wish to see it again … Caneletto's pictures please me far better, inasmuch as I cannot in them smell these most stinking canals.

But by the end of a later visit to the city (1865) even he had to admit that, 'Against my will no place has so impressed me – ever.' Being impressed by a place isn't quite the same as loving it, however … as the following writers, or the characters they create, clearly do. In the 'Foreword' to her novel, Pippa Passes, Rumer Godden admits that Venice isn't for everyone but tells how she came to love the city.

It seems, for travellers nowadays, there are two Venices, both extreme – she is not a city of mediocrity. For many, her strange rich history, her treasures, the beauty of her churches, palaces, tall houses with their blending colours, the fascination of her waterways are overlaid by the decay, stale smells and filth, with the overpress of tourists, extortionate prices, the unfriendliness – I should say reserve – of her inhabitants unless you have money. These poor visitors do not even notice the famous, ever-changing translucent Venetian light; her magic is not for them.

Others, perhaps now only a few, are captivated. Long after they leave they will remember that light; remember, too, hidden canals with gardens and houses which tourists seldom see – the canals are too narrow for the *vaporetti*, water ferries, to use and gondolas are ludicrously expensive. I would, though, sacrifice a great deal to go in a gondola, particularly at night when one can hear the lapping of the water round the boat, the gondolier's cry of '*Ohé*' as he rounds the corners. They will remember churches, big and little, the great piazza San Marco with its winged lion on its pillar, the pigeons, the café music and other small, tucked-away *campielli* and squares, the markets – and the romance.

By good fortune I had had my eyes opened to Venice long before I saw her.

I must have been in my late teens when, in one of the second-hand bookshops I haunted in the Sussex town where I was born, I picked up a book, heavy, bound in green cloth, lettered in gold. It was by E. Temple Thurston. [...]

I bought the book and read it; even then I recognized how unashamedly sentimental it was – novels were sentimental at the turn of the century and this was a love story – but, in spite of that, its evocation of Venice cast such a spell that it has been with me ever since. Though I fully admit the truths of her detractors, I feel that spell again every time I go there, not just the spell of her riches but of Venice herself – unique, Venice *serenissima*, and I yield myself to her.

Rumer Godden, *Pippa Passes* (1994)

✳ ✳ ✳

The narrator of Susan Hill's The Man in the Picture *starts out as a devotee – even if events take a sinister turn as the novel progresses ... .*

Venice is beautiful. Venice is magical. Venice is like nowhere else, in the real world or the worlds of invention. I remembered the first time I visited it, as a young man taking a few months out to travel, and emerging from the railway station to that astonishing sight – streets which were water. The first ride on the vaporetto down the Grand Canal, the first glimpse of San Giorgio Maggiore rising out of the mist, the first sight of the pigeons rising like a ghostly cloud above the cathedral in St Mark's Square, and of those turrets and spires touched with gold and gleaming in the sun. Walks through squares where all you hear are the sounds of many footsteps on stone, because there are no motor vehicles, hours spent at café tables on the quiet Giudecca, the cry of the fish-sellers in the early morning, the graceful arch of the Rialto Bridge, the faces of the locals, old and young men and women with those memorable, ancient Venetian features – the prominent nose, the hauteur of expression, the red hair.

The more I thought about the city in those days leading up to the wedding, the more my pulse quickened with the anticipation of seeing it again, and this time with Anne. Venice filled my dreams and was there when I woke. I found myself searching out books about her – the novels by Henry James and Edith Wharton and others which caught the moods so vividly.

Susan Hill, *The Man in the Picture* (2007)

✻ ✻ ✻

And two non-fictional responses to the city – letters from English poet Elizabeth Barrett Browning (1806–61) and French novelist George Sand (1804–1876).

I have been between heaven and earth since our arrival in Venice. The heaven of it is ineffable. Never had I touched the skirts of so celestial a place. The beauty of the architecture, the silver trails of water up between all that gorgeous colour and carving, the enchanting silence, the moonlight, the music, the gondolas – I mix it all up together, and maintain that nothing is like it, nothing equal to it, not a second Venice in the world. Do you know, when I came first I felt as if I never could go away. But now comes the earth side. Robert, after sharing the ecstasy, grows uncomfortable, and nervous, and unable to eat or sleep; and poor Wilson, still worse, in a miserable condition of continual sickness and headache. Alas for these mortal Venices – so exquisite and so bilious! Therefore I am constrained away from my joys by sympathy, and am forced to be glad that we are going off on Friday. For myself, it does not affect me at all. I like these moist, soft, relaxing climates; even the sirocco doesn't touch me much. And the baby grows gloriously fatter in spite of everything.

Elizabeth Barrett Browning, letter to Mary Russell Mitford, 1851

✻ ✻ ✻

No-one has ever adequately described the beauty of the heavens, nor the pleasures of night-time Venice. So calm is the lagoon that, on fine evenings, there is not even any trembling of the stars upon its surface. When you are in the middle of it, it is so blue, so silent, and one cannot even identify the line of the horizon as the water and the sky form a veil of azure blue, where even day-dreaming loses itself and falls asleep. The atmosphere is so transparent, so pure, that thousands more stars are visible than we can see in Northern France. Here I have seen nights when the silvery glimmer of stars took up more space in the firmament than the blue of the night sky between them – a galaxy of diamonds casting almost as strong a light as a Parisian moon ... Here Nature, maybe more powerful in her influence, forces too much silence upon the mind, putting all thoughts to sleep but stirring the heart and ruling the senses. Unless one is a genius, one must not even dream of writing poetry during these voluptuous nights: one must either love or sleep.

George Sand, *Lettres d'un voyageur* (1857)
translated by E. King

* * *

And American Henry James on the simple charms of the place ...

It is charming to wander through the light and shade of intricate canals, with perpetual architecture above you and perpetual fluidity beneath. It is charming to disembark at the polished steps of a little empty *campo* – a sunny shabby square with an old well in the middle, an old church on one side and tall Venetian windows looking down.

Henry James, *Italian Hours* (1909)

* * *

Born in Venice in 1707, famous playwright Carlo Goldoni never lost his appreciation of his native city's beauty and uniqueness.

Venice is such an extraordinary city that it isn't possible to form a proper idea of what it's like without having seen it. Maps, plans, models, descriptions – none of them suffice: you have to see it. All the world's cities resemble each other to a greater or lesser degree: this one is like none of them. Each time I saw it again, after a long absence, it surprised me anew. [...]

If you enter from the San Marco side – past a vast array of all kinds of buildings, as well as war ships, merchant ships, frigates, galleys, boats big and small, along with gondolas – you set foot upon a waterside area called 'la Piazzetta' (the little square) where ysou see, to one side, the Doges' palace and church, which proclaim the magnificence of the Republic; and to the other side, the Piazza San Marco, bordered by raised arcades built to designs by Palladio and Sansovino. You go via the little shopping streets as far as the Rialto bridge, walking upon cobbles of Istrian marble dotted with indentations to prevent them from being slippery; you go through a locale that seems like a perpetual fairground, and you arrive at that bridge which, with a single arch ninety feet wide, crosses the Grand Canal, and which, because of its height, allows quite big boats to pass beneath it, even at high tide, and which offers three different paths to those crossing it on foot, and which supports on its curve twenty-four proper, lead-roofed shops.

Carlo Goldoni, *Memoirs* (1787)
translated by E. F. Morgan

* * *

Donna Leon's fictional Venetian, Police Commissioner Guido Brunetti, reveals why he loves his city most at night.

Brunetti walked up towards the hotel, still lighted, even at this hour when the rest of the city was darkened and sleeping. Once the capital of the dissipations of a continent, Venice had become a sleepy provincial town that virtually ceased to exist after nine or ten at night. During the summer months, she could remember her courtesan past and sparkle, as long as the tourists paid and the good weather held, but in the winter, she became a tired old crone, eager to crawl early to bed, leaving her deserted streets to cats and memories of the past.

But these were the hours when, for Brunetti, the city became most beautiful, just as they were the same hours when he, Venetian to the bone, could sense some of her past glory. The darkness of the night hid the moss that crept up the steps of the *palazzi* lining the Grand Canal, obscured the cracks in the walls of churches, and covered the patches of plaster missing from the façades of public buildings. Like many women of a certain age, the city needed the help of deceptive light to recapture her vanished beauty. A boat that, during the day, was making a delivery of soap powder or cabbages, at night became a numinous form, floating towards some mysterious destination. The fogs that were common in these winter days could transform people and objects, even turn long-haired teenagers, hanging around a street corner and sharing a cigarette, into mysterious phantoms from the past.

He glanced up at the stars, seen clearly above the darkness of the unlighted street, and noticed their beauty. Holding their image in mind, he continued towards the hotel.

Donna Leon, *Death at La Fenice* (1992)

✼ ✼ ✼

Visiting Venice after a long absence, one can be struck afresh by the place's beauty – and the pleasure of a city without the hurly-burly of traffic.

We swept in the course of five minutes into the Grand Canal; whereupon she uttered a murmur of ecstasy as fresh as if she had been a tourist just arrived. She had forgotten the splendour of the great water-way on a clear summer evening, and how the sense of floating between marble palaces and reflected lights disposed the mind to freedom and ease. We floated long and far, and though my friend gave no high-pitched voice to her glee I was sure of her full surrender. She was more than pleased, she was transported; the whole thing was an immense liberation. The gondola moved with slow strokes, to give her time to enjoy it, and she listened to the plash of the oars, which grew louder and more musically liquid as we passed into narrow canals, as if it were a revelation of Venice. When I asked her how long it was since she had thus floated she answered: 'Oh I don't know; a long time – not since my aunt began to be ill.' This was not the only show of her extreme vagueness about the previous years and the line marking off the period of Miss Bordereau's eminence. I was not at liberty to keep her out long, but we took a considerable *giro* before going to the Piazza. I asked her no questions, holding off by design from her life at home and the things I wanted to know; I poured, rather, treasures of information about the objects before and around us into her ears, describing also Florence and Rome, discoursing on the charms and advantages of travel. She reclined, receptive, on the deep leather cushions, turned her eyes conscientiously to everything I noted and never mentioned to me till some time afterwards that she might be supposed to know Florence better than I, as she had lived there for years with her kinswoman. At last she said with the shy impatience of a child. 'Are we not really going to the Piazza? That's what I want to see!' I immediately gave the order that we should go straight, after which we sat silent with the expectation of arrival. [...]

The gondola approached the Piazzetta. After we had disembarked I asked my companion if she would rather walk round the square or go and sit before the great café; to which she replied that she would do whichever I liked best – I must only remember again how little time she had. I assured her there was plenty to do both, and we made the circuit of the long arcades. Her spirits revived at the sight of the bright shop-windows, and she lingered and stopped, admiring or disapproving of their contents, asking me what I thought of things, theorising about prices. My attention wandered from her; her words of a while before 'Oh she has everything!' echoed so in my consciousness. We sat down at last in the crowded circle at Florian's, finding an unoccupied table among those that were ranged in the square. It was a splendid night and all the world out-of-doors; Miss Tina couldn't have wished the elements more auspicious for her return to society. I saw she felt it all even more than she told, but her impressions were well-nigh too many for her. She had forgotten the attraction of the world and was learning that she had for the best years of her life been rather mercilessly cheated of it. This didn't make her angry; but as she took in the charming scene her face had, in spite of its smile of appreciation, the flush of a wounded surprise. [...]

I don't know why it happened that on this occasion I was more than ever struck with that queer air of sociability, of cousinship and family life, which makes up half the expression of Venice. Without streets and vehicles, the uproar of wheels, the brutality of horses, and with its little winding ways where people crowd together, where voices sound as in the corridors of a house, where the human step circulates as if it skirted the angles of furniture and shoes never wear out, the place has the character of an immense collective apartment, in which Piazza San Marco is the most ornamented corner and palaces and churches, for the rest, play the part of great divans of repose, tables of entertainment, expanses of decoration. And somehow the splendid common domicile, familiar domestic and resonant, also resembles a theatre with its actors clicking over bridges and, in straggling processions, tripping along fondamentas. As you sit in your gondola the footways that in certain parts edge the canals assume to the eye the importance of a stage, meeting it at the same angle, and the Venetian figures, moving to and fro against the battered scenery of their little houses of comedy, strike you as members of an endless dramatic troupe.

Henry James, *The Aspern Papers* (1888)

❊ ❊ ❊

As for Henry James, some of the pleasures of the city for contemporary visitor, Bidisha, are to be found in

*the people – the way they behave, the way they dress,
the way they relate to each other.*

Over the next ten days we establish a routine: coffee at a
different sugary-smelling *pasticceria* (dainty cake 'n' coffee
place), standing at the counter while all around me slim, tall,
soigné natives choose from the dozens of bite-size delicacies on
display. Then we meet Ginevra for a day of sights and walks
followed by an aperitif at an *osteria*. I'm woken every morning
by the sound of water and of boats going by, boatmen's cries,
pearlescent light. As a general rule, Ginevra and Stefania speak
to me in English, as do her parents; everything else happens in
Italian. There is a certain poised Venetian way of doing things, I
notice, and when we're in our group of three girls we are treated
with unremitting gallantry, efficiency and clarity by everyone
we encounter. Shopping and eating are to be done lightly, casu-
ally, not greedily; conversation is lively but not sleazy; vulgarity
is frowned upon, moderation rewarded. Coffee is to be drunk
during the day, good wine at night. And one must always be
well dressed, otherwise social ostracism will follow. We have
our own café, Caffè Rosso in Campo Santa Margherita, and
our own bar/eats place, La Cantina on the Strada Nova. I can
order a cup of coffee and understand about half of what I'm
hearing, until someone addresses me directly.

For the first few days everything looks the same: the bridges,
the alleys and sunny dusty squares, the shops all selling things for
the body, if not shoes and clothes then bags, scarves, brooches,
underwear, gloves. Dickens described Venice as being coiled,
wound, turned in on itself like a spring. Not true. In fact, everything is spliced and stacked upright and then sprinkled with
roof tiles. The map makes it all look like soft curve, a yin-yang
melting in the sea, but once you're on the streets, squashed in
amongst the houses and turning left and right randomly, you're
like a mouse in a box of old books. The buildings only get taller,
squarer, darker, flatter and more identical. To get away from this

in between museum visits, I linger on benches by the two coasts or along the banks of the Canal Grande. Record the differences: water that sounds like laughter, water that sounds like keys or chains or shingle, water that sounds like a gunshot, water like an echo. I can never tell what things are here, bells or engines or voices, children or birds, water or machines, the noises reflect and change. The sound of a boat's engine is one single note deep in the water and sounds like a chair scraping across the floor.

One morning Stefania and Ginevra take me down to San Polo in the middle of Venice, on the other side of Rialto Bridge (what I think of as the other half of the biscuit), where the streets are narrower, churchy, crooked and dank and secretive. The stalls of Rialto market are garish with cheap clothes and 'Venezia'-logo sweatshirts, imported leather wallets and fruit stalls offering slices of watermelon, tubs of strawberries and segments of coconut for drooping visitors. We see a group of kids and parents walking out from a school – and this is a notable thing, the visibility and respect given to family life, resulting directly in the boisterous, charming, unafraid children themselves.

Bidisha, *Venetian Masters* (2008)

* * *

One of Venice's most famous visitors from the past, Goethe, begins his Venice diary with comments on the people of the city, but goes on to describe a place that, over two hundred years later, is still recognisably the same.

So much has been said and written about Venice already that I do not want to describe it too minutely. I shall only give my immediate impression. What strikes me most is again the people in their sheer mass and instinctive existence.

This race did not seek refuge in these islands for fun, nor were those who joined later moved by chance; necessity taught them to find safety in the most unfavourable location. Later, however, this turned out to their greatest advantage and made them wise at a time when the whole northern world still lay in darkness; their increasing population and wealth were a logical consequence. Houses were crowded closer and closer together, sand and swamp transformed into solid pavement. The houses grew upward like closely planted trees and were forced to make up in height for what they were denied in width. Avid for every inch of ground and cramped into a narrow space from the very beginning, they kept the alleys separating two rows of houses narrow, just wide enough to let people pass each other. The place of street and square and promenade was taken by water. In consequence, the Venetian was bound to develop into a new kind of creature, and that is why, too, Venice can only be compared to itself. The Canal Grande, winding snakelike through the town, is unlike any other street in the world, and no square can compete with the vast expanse of water in front of the Piazza San Marco, enclosed on one side by the semicircle of Venice itself. Across it to the left is the island of San Giorgio Maggiore, to the right the Guidecca with its canal, and still further to the right the Dogana with the entrance to the Canal Grande, where stand some great gleaming marble temples. These, in brief, are the chief objects which strike the eye when one leaves the Piazza San Marco between the two columns.

After dinner I hurried out without a guide and, after noting the four points of the compass, plunged into the labyrinth of this city, which is intersected everywhere by canals but joined together by bridges. The compactness of it all is unimaginable unless one has seen it. As a rule, one can measure the width of an alley with one's outstretched arms; in the narrowest, one even scrapes one's elbows if one holds them akimbo; occasionally there is a wider lane and even a little square every so often, but everything is relatively narrow.

I easily found the Canal Grande and its principal bridge, the Ponte Rialto, which is a single arch of white marble. Looking down, I saw the Canal teeming with gondolas and the barges which bring all necessities from the mainland and land at this point to unload. As today is the Feast of St Michael, the scene was especially full of life.

The Canal Grande, which separates the two main islands of Venice, is only spanned by a single bridge, the Rialto, but it can be crossed in open boats at various points. Today I watched with delight as many well-dressed women in black veils were ferried across on their way to the Church of the Solemnized Archangel. I left the bridge and walked to one of the landing points to get a closer look at them as they left the ferry. There were some beautiful faces and figures among them.

When I felt tired, I left the narrow alleys and took my seat in a gondola. Wishing to enjoy the view from the opposite side, I passed the northern end of the Canal Grande, round the island of Santa Chiara, into the lagoons, then into the Giudecca Canal and continued as far as the Piazza San Marco. Reclining in my gondola, I suddenly felt myself, as every Venetian does, a lord of the Adriatic. I thought with piety of my father, for nothing gave him greater pleasure than to talk of these things. It will be the same with me, I know. Everything around me is a worthy, stupendous monument, not to one ruler, but to a whole people. Their lagoons may be gradually silting up and unhealthy miasmas hovering over their marshes, their trade may be declining, their political power dwindling, but this republic will never become a whit less vulnerable in the eyes of one observer. Venice, like everything else which has a phenomenal existence, is subject to Time.

30 September

Towards evening I explored – again without a guide – the remoter quarters of the city. All the bridges are provided with stairs, so that gondolas and even larger boats can pass under their arches without difficulty. I tried to find my way in and out of the labyrinth by myself, asking nobody the way and taking my directions only from the points of the compass. It is possible to do this and I find my method of personal experience the best. I have been to the furthest edges of the inhabited area and studied the way of life, the morals and manners of the inhabitants. They are different in every district. Good heavens! What a poor good creature man is after all.

Many little houses rise directly from the canals, but here and there are well-paved footpaths on which one can stroll very pleasantly between water, churches and palaces. One agreeable walk is along the stone quay on the northern side. From it one can see the smaller islands, among them Murano, a Venice in miniature. The intervening lagoons are alive with innumerable gondolas.

Evening

Today I bought a map of the city. After studying it carefully, I climbed the Campanile of San Marco. It was nearly noon and the sun shone so brightly that I could recognize both close and distant places without a telescope. The lagoons are covered at high tide, and when I turned my eyes in the direction of the Lido, a narrow strip of land which shuts in the lagoons, I saw the sea for the first time. Some sails were visible on it, and in the lagoons themselves galleys and frigates were lying at anchor. These were to have joined Admiral Emo, who is fighting the Algerians, but unfavourable winds have detained them here. North and west, the hills of Padua and Vicenza and the Tirolean Alps made a beautiful frame to the whole picture.

1 October

Today was Sunday, and as I walked about I was struck by the uncleanliness of the streets. This set me thinking. There appears to be some kind of police regulation on this matter, for people sweep the rubbish into corners and I saw large barges stopping at certain points and carrying the rubbish away. They came from the surrounding islands where people are in need of manure. But there is no logic or discipline in these arrangements. The dirt is all the more inexcusable because the city is as designed for cleanliness as any Dutch town. All the street are paved with flagstones; even in the remotest quarter, bricks are at least placed on the kerb and, wherever it is necessary, the streets are raised in the middle and have gutters at their sides to catch the water and carry it off into covered drains. These and other technical devices are clearly the work of efficient architects who planned to make Venice the cleanest of cities as well as the most unusual.

Johann Wolfgang von Goethe, *Italian Journey [1786–1788]*
translated by W. H. Auden and Elizabeth Mayer

✳ ✳ ✳

A nineteenth-century visitor, American writer Mark Twain, begins with a humorously disappointed experience of the city. But then, in the moonlight, everything changes …

We reached Venice at eight in the evening, and entered a hearse belonging to the Grand Hotel d'Europe. At any rate, it was more like a hearse than anything else, though, to speak by the card, it was a gondola. And this was the storied gondola of Venice! – the fairy boat in which the princely cavaliers of the olden time were wont to cleave the waters of the moonlit canals and look the eloquence of love into the soft eyes of patrician beauties, while the gay gondolier in silken doublet touched his guitar and sang as only gondoliers can sing! This the famed gondola and this the gorgeous gondolier! – the one an inky, rusty old canoe with a sable hearse-body clapped on to the middle of it, and the other a mangy, barefooted gutter-snipe with a portion of his raiment on exhibition which should have been sacred from public scrutiny. Presently, as he turned a corner and shot his hearse into a dismal ditch between two long rows of towering, untenanted buildings, the gay gondolier began to sing, true to the tradition of his race. I stood it a little while. Then I said:

'Now, here, Roderigo Gonzales Michael Angelo, I'm a pilgrim, and I'm a stranger, but I am not going to have my feelings lacerated by any such caterwauling as that. If that goes on, one of us has got to take water. It is enough that my cherished dreams of Venice have been blighted forever as to the romantic gondola and the gorgeous gondolier; this system of destruction shall go no farther; I will accept the hearse, under protest, and you may fly your flag of truce in peace, but here I register a dark and bloody oath that you shan't sing. Another yelp, and overboard you go.'

I began to feel that the old Venice of song and story had departed forever. But I was too hasty. In a few minutes we swept gracefully out into the Grand Canal, and under the mellow moonlight the Venice of poetry and romance stood revealed. Right from the water's edge rose long lines of stately palaces of marble; gondolas were gliding swiftly hither and thither and disappearing suddenly through unsuspected gates and alleys; ponderous stone bridges threw their shadows athwart the glittering waves. There was life and motion everywhere, and yet everywhere there was a hush, a stealthy sort of stillness, that was suggestive of secret enterprises of bravoes and of lovers; and, clad half in moonbeams and half in mysterious shadows, the grim old mansions of the Republic seemed to have an expression about them of having an eye out for just such enterprises as these at that same moment. Music came floating over waters – Venice was complete.

Mark Twain, *The Innocents Abroad* (1869)

* * *

Expert on Venice, novelist Henry James admits that Venice isn't always easy to live in and that one can get thoroughly tired of it all. But then the city works its magic …

The Venice of to-day is a vast museum where the little wicket that admits you is perpetually turning and creaking, and you march through the institution with a herd of fellow-gazers.

There is nothing left to discover or describe, and originality of attitude is completely impossible. This is often very annoying; you can only turn your back on your impertinent playfellow and curse his want of delicacy. But this is not the fault of Venice; it is the fault of the rest of the world. The fault of Venice is that, though she is easy to admire, she is not so easy to live with as you count living in other places. After you have stayed a week and the bloom of novelty has rubbed off you wonder if you can accommodate yourself to the peculiar conditions. Your old habits become impracticable and you find yourself obliged to form new ones of an undesirable and unprofitable character. You are tired of your gondola (or you think you are) and you have seen all the principal pictures and heard the names of the palaces announced a dozen times by your gondolier, who brings them out almost as impressively as if he were an English butler bawling titles into a drawing-room. You have walked several hundred times round the Piazza and bought several bushels of photographs. You have visited the antiquity mongers whose horrible sign-boards dishonour some of the grandest vistas in the Grand Canal; you have tried the opera and found it very bad; you have bathed at the Lido and found the water flat. You have begun to have a shipboard-feeling – to regard the Piazza as an enormous saloon and the Riva degli Schiavoni as a promenade-deck. You are obstructed and encaged; your desire for space is unsatisfied; you miss your usual exercise. You try to take a walk and you fail, and meantime, as I say, you have come to regard your gondola as a sort of magnified baby's cradle. You have no desire to be rocked to sleep, though you are sufficiently kept awake by the irritation produced, as you gaze across the shallow lagoon, by the attitude of the perpetual gondolier, with his turned-out toes, his protruded chin, his absurdly unscientific stroke. The canals have a horrible smell, and the everlasting Piazza, where you have looked repeatedly at every article in every shop-window and found them all rubbish, where the young Venetians who sell bead bracelets and "pano-ramas" are perpetually thrusting their wares at you, where the same tightly-buttoned officers are for ever sucking the same black weeds, at the same empty tables, in front of the same cafes – the Piazza, as I say, has resolved itself into a magnificent tread-mill. This is the state of mind of those shallow inquirers who find Venice all very well for a week; and if in such a state of mind you take your departure you act with fatal rashness. The loss is your own, moreover; it is not – with all deference to your personal attractions – that of your companions who remain behind; for though there are some disagreeable things in Venice there is nothing so disagreeable as the visitors. The conditions are peculiar, but your intolerance of them evapo-rates before it has had time to become a prejudice. When you have called for the bill to go, pay it and remain, and you will find on the morrow that you are deeply attached to Venice. It is by living there from day to day that you feel the fulness of her charm; that you invite her exquisite influence to sink into your spirit. [...]

Certain little mental pictures rise before the collector of memories at the simple mention, written or spoken, of the places he has loved. When I hear, when I see, the magical name I have written above these pages, it is not of the great Square that I think, with its strange basilica and its high arcades, nor of the wide mouth of the Grand Canal, with the stately steps and the well-poised dome of the Salute; it is not of the low lagoon, nor the sweet Piazzetta, nor the dark chambers of St Mark's. I simply see a narrow canal in the heart of the city – a patch of green water and a surface of pink wall. The gondola moves slowly; it gives a great smooth swerve, passes under a bridge, and the gondolier's cry, carried over the quiet water, makes a kind of splash in the stillness. A girl crosses the little bridge, which has an arch like a camel's back, with an old shawl on her head, which makes her characteristic and charming; you

43

see her against the sky as you float beneath. The pink of the old wall seems to fill the whole place; it sinks even into the opaque water. Behind the wall is a garden, out of which the long arm of a white June rose – the roses of Venice are splendid – has flung itself by way of spontaneous ornament. On the other side of this small water-way is a great shabby façade of Gothic windows and balconies – balconies on which dirty clothes are hung and under which a cavernous-looking doorway opens from a low flight of slimy water-steps. It is very hot and still, the canal has a queer smell, and the whole place is enchanting. [...]

Certain lovely mornings of May and June come back with an ineffaceable fairness. Venice isn't smothered in flowers at this season, in the manner of Florence and Rome; but the sea and sky themselves seem to blossom and rustle. The gondola waits at the wave-washed steps, and if you are wise you will take your place beside a discriminating companion. Such a companion in Venice should of course be of the sex that discriminates most finely. An intelligent woman who knows her Venice seems doubly intelligent, and it makes no woman's perceptions less keen to be aware that she can't help looking graceful as she is borne over the waves. The handsome Pasquale, with uplifted oar, awaits your command, knowing, in a general way, from observation of your habits, that your intention is to go to see a picture or two. It perhaps doesn't immensely matter what picture you choose: the whole affair is so charming. It is charming to wander through the light and shade of intricate canals, with perpetual architecture above you and perpetual fluidity beneath. It is charming to disembark at the polished steps of a little empty *campo* – a sunny shabby square with an old well in the middle, an old church on one side and tall Venetian windows looking down. Sometimes the windows are tenantless; sometimes a lady in a faded dressing-gown leans vaguely on the sill. There is always an old man holding out his hat for coppers; there are always three or four small boys dodging possible umbrella-pokes while they precede you, in the manner of custodians, to the door of the church.

Henry James, *Italian Hours* (1909)

*　*　*

For Marcel Proust, part of the pleasure of Venice is the way it evokes memories of his early life.

My mother had taken me to spend a few weeks in Venice, and – as beauty may exist in the most precious as well as in the humblest things – I received there impressions analogous to those which I had felt so often in the past at Combray, but transposed into a wholly different and far richer key. When, at ten o'clock in the morning, my shutters were thrown open, I saw blazing there, instead of the gleaming black marble into which the slates of Saint-Hilaire used to turn, the golden angel on the campanile of St Mark's. Glittering in a sunlight which made it almost impossible to keep one's eyes upon it, this angel promised me, with its outstretched arms, for the moment when I appeared on the Piazzetta half an hour later, a joy more certain than any that it could ever in the past have been bidden to announce to men of good will. I could see nothing else so long as I remained in bed, but as the whole world is merely a vast sundial, a single sunlit segment of which enables us to tell what time it is, on the very first morning I was reminded of the shops in the Place de l'Eglise at Combray, which, on Sunday mornings, were always on the point of shutting when I arrived for mass, while the straw in the market-place smelt strongly in the already hot sunlight. But on the second morning, what I saw on awakening, what made me get out of bed (because they had taken the place in my memory and in my desire of the recollections of Combray), were the impressions of my first morning stroll in Venice, in Venice where everyday life was no less real than in Combray, where as in Combray on Sunday mornings one had the pleasure of stepping down into a festive street, but where that street was entirely paved with sapphire-blue water, cooled by warm breezes and of a colour so durable that my tired eyes might rest their gaze upon it in search of relaxation without fear of its blenching. Like the good folk of the Rue de l'Oiseau at Combry, so also in this strange town, the inhabitants actually emerged from houses lined up side by side along the main street, but the role played there by houses of casting a patch of shade at their feet was entrusted in Venice to palaces of porphyry and jasper, above the arched doors of which the head of a beaded god (breaking the alignment, like the knocker on a door at Combray) had the effect of darkening with its shadow, not the brownness of the earth, but the splendid blueness of the water. On the Piazza, the shadow that would have been produced at Combray by the awning over the draper's shop and the barber's pole was a carpet of little blue flowers strewn at its feet upon the desert of sun-scorched flagstones by the relief of a Renaissance façade, which is not to say that, when the sun beat down, one was not obliged, in Venice as at Combray, to pull down the blinds, even beside the canal, but they hung between the quatrefoils and foliage of Gothic windows.

Marcel Proust, *The Fugitive* (1925)
translated by C. K. Scott Moncrieff and Terence Kilmartin

* * *

Venetian Paolo Barbaro's love of his home city oozes from every sentence of this brief description of a Venetian morning.

Another limpid morning. By noon there's a kind of chaotic double exposure of light on the houses, the boats, the taverns, the passersby with their staring, pitiless eyes (who are you, who do you think you are?), the hundreds and thousands of lives brushing by you on the banks of Venice, in the streets of Venice, some of them – calli, rive, windows, people, lives – of super-human beauty. From the shores of the Giudecca to the Punta della Dogana there is a dance of coloured dust motes, of water flowing beneath them and yearning toward them, of tiny, unbelievably luminous wavelets, of marble reflecting and returning its reflections – an incredible rock 'n' roll of slivers of sea-earth-light, all moving in perfect freedom between the old columns of the Dogana. The boys on the bank are no longer fishing; they're running, they're flying. Where is the customs officers' house? Ah, it's tucked away behind here, dozing among the centuries, lying tranquil in the sun, washed clean of its ghosts.

Paolo Barbaro, *Venice Revealed* (1998)
translated by Tami Calliope

✳ ✳ ✳

*It's all too easy to fall under the spell of Venice, from
the sunlit water to Harry's Bar ...*

The fortnight at Venice passed quickly and sweetly – perhaps too sweetly; I was drowning in honey, stingless. On some days life kept pace with the gondola, as we nosed through the side-canals and the boatman uttered his plaintive musical bird-cry of warning; on other days with the speed-boat bouncing over the lagoon in a stream of sun-lit foam; it left a confused memory of fierce sunlight on the sands and cool, marble interiors; of water everywhere, lapping on smooth stone, reflected in a dapple of light on painted ceilings; of a night at the Corombona palace such as Byron might have known, and another Byronic night fishing for scampi in the shallows of Choggia, the phosphorescent wake of the little ship, the lantern swinging in the prow, and the net coming up full of weed and sand and floundering fishes; of melon and *prosciutto* on the balcony in the cool of the morning; of hot cheese sandwiches and champagne cocktails at Harry's Bar.

Evelyn Waugh, *Brideshead Revisited* (1945)

47

* * *

And John Berendt sums up the reasons why it's so easy to love Venice.

I had been to Venice a dozen times or more, having fallen under her spell when I first caught sight of it twenty years before – a city of domes and bell towers, floating hazily in the distance, topped here and there by a marble saint or a gilded angel. [...]

To me Venice was not merely beautiful: it was beautiful everywhere. On one occasion I set about testing this notion by concocting a game called 'photo roulette', the object of which was to walk around the city taking photographs at unplanned moments – whenever a church bell rang or at every sighting of a dog or cat – to see how often, standing at an arbitrary spot, one would be confronted by a view of exceptional beauty. The answer: almost always. [...]

Why Venice?

Because, to my mind, Venice was uniquely beautiful, isolated, inward-looking, and a powerful stimulant to the senses, the intellect, and the imagination.

Because, despite its miles of tangled streets and canals, Venice was a lot smaller and more manageable than it seemed at first. At eighteen hundred acres, in fact, Venice was barely twice the size of Central Park.

Because I had always found the sound of church bells pealing every fifteen minutes – close at hand and distant, solo and in concert, each with its own persona – a tonic to the ears and nerves.

Because I could not imagine a more enticing beat to assign myself for an indefinite period of time.

And because, if the worst-case scenario for the rising sea level were to be believed, Venice might not be there very long.

John Berendt, *City of Falling Angels* (2005)

Some unmissable places

In a city of so many riches, how do you decide what's unmissable and what isn't? Impossible! Venetian Tiziano Scarpa leads us into his city ... and suggests throwing away your map.

Venice is a fish. Just look at it on a map. It's like a vast sole stretched out against the deep. How did this marvellous beast make its way up the Adriatic and fetch up here, of all places? It could set off on its travels at any time, it could call in just about anywhere, following its fancy: it could migrate, travel, frolic as it has always liked to do. Dalmatia this weekend, Istanbul the day after next, summer in Cyprus. If it's anchored hereabouts, there must be a reason for it. Salmon wear themselves out swimming against the current, climbing waterfalls to make love in the mountains. Sirens and swordfish and seahorses go to the Sargasso Sea to die.

Other books would laugh at what I'm telling you. They speak of the birth of the city from nothing, its resounding commercial and military success, its decadence: poppycock. It wasn't like that, believe me. Venice has always existed as you see it today, more or less. It's been sailing since the dawn of time; it's put in at every port, it's rubbed up against every shore, quay and landing-stage: Middle Eastern pearls, transparent Phoenician sand, Greek seashells, Byzantine seaweed all accreted on its scales. But one day it felt all the weight of those scales, those fragments and splinters that had permanently accumulated on its skin; it felt the weight of the incrustations it was carrying around. Its flippers grew too heavy to slip among the currents. It decided to climb once and for all into one of the most northerly and sheltered inlets of the Mediterranean, and rest there.

On the map, the bridge connecting it to terra firma looks like a fishing-line: Venice looks as if it's swallowed the bait. It's doubly bound: a steel platform and a strip of tarmac; but that happened afterwards, just a century ago. We were worried that Venice might one day change its mind and go off travelling again; we fastened it to the lagoon so that it wouldn't suddenly get it into its head to weigh anchor and leave, this time forever. We tell everyone else we did it for its own protection, because after all those years in its moorings, it's lost the knack of swimming: it would be caught straight away, it would end up on some Japanese whaling ship, or on display in a Disneyland aquarium. The truth is that we can no longer do without it. We're jealous. And even sadistic and violent, when it comes to keeping someone we love. We've done something worse than tying it to terra firma: we've literally nailed it to the sea bed. [...]

These buildings that you see, the marble *palazzi*, the brick houses, couldn't have been built on water, they would have sunk into the mud. How do you lay solid foundations on slime? The Venetians thrust hundreds of thousands, millions of poles into the lagoon. Underneath the Basilica della Salute there are at least a hundred thousand; and also at the feet of the Rialto Bridge, to support the thrust of the stone arch. St Mark's Basilica rests on big oaken rafts, supported by elm-wood stilts. The trunks were floated down to the lagoon along the River Piave, from the Selva di Cadore on the slopes of the Venetian Alps. There are larches, elms, alders, pines and oaks. La Serenissima was very shrewd, she always kept a close eye on her wooden possessions, the forests were protected by laws of draconian severity.

Upside-down trees, hammered in with a kind of anvil hoisted on pulleys. I had the chance to see them as a child: I heard the songs of the pile-drivers, sung to the rhythm of the slow and powerful percussion of those cylindrical mallets suspended in the air, running on vertical rails, slowly rising and then crashing back down again. The trunks are mineralised precisely because of the mud, which has wrapped them in its protective sheath, preventing them from rotting in contact with oxygen: breathless for centuries, the wood has been turned almost to stone.

You're walking on a vast upside-down forest, strolling above an incredible inverted wood. It's like something dreamed up by a mediocre science-fiction writer, and yet it's true. [...]

Where are you going? Throw away your map! Why do you so desperately need to know where you are right now? OK: in all cities, in the commercial centres, at bus stops or underground stations, you're used to having signs that hold you by the hand; there's almost always a big map with a coloured dot, an arrow to bellow at you, 'You are here'. In Venice, too, you need only look up to see lots of yellow signs with arrows telling you: you've got to go this way, don't get confused, *To the Railway Station, To San Marco, To the Accademia*. Forget it, just ignore them. Why fight the labyrinth? Follow it, for once. Don't worry, let the streets decide your journey for you, rather than the other way round. Learn to wander, to dawdle. Lose your bearings. Just drift.

Tiziano Scarpa, *Venice is a Fish* (2000)
translated by Shaun Whiteside

❊ ❊ ❊

A fictional character – Mary in Jane Langton's The
Thief of Venice (one of her Homer Kelly mystery
stories) – starts off with a guidebook, but she, too,
ends up "wandering without direction" as she
attempts to capture as much of the city as possible
with her camera.

Mary got up early and prepared for another day of exploration. She stuck her folding umbrella in her bag along with her
guidebook, her pocket dictionary, a sandwich, and a mirror and
comb. Tucked into her billfold were her Venetian phone card, a
slip entitling her to one more visit to the toilet near San Marco,
and her *abbonamento*, the ticket that allowed her freedom of
travel on the Grand Canal, anywhere, any time, by vaporetto.

First stop, the Accademia, because Venice was a city of
painters. Here Mary would find them all assembled – the three
Bellinis, Carpaccio, Giogione, Titian, Tintoretto, Tiepolo,
Veronese, Lotto, Guardi, Canaletto! There was no end to the
supply of great Venetian painters. They had set each other off,
one skyrocket igniting another.

But when she stepped down from the vaporetto, she was too
early for the Accademia. It would not open for hours. Listlessly
she bought a paper at the kiosk and sat down on a bench.
Newspaper Italian was easy to guess at. There was a murder on
the front page, but it meant nothing to Mary Kelly. Gloomily
she tossed the paper in a trash basket, and looked mournfully
at the palaces across the Grand Canal.

Church bells were bonging. From somewhere came the
piping bark of a dog. A gull floated in and out of the sunlight.
She was homesick.

Oh, it was so stupid. Here she was in this most ravishing of
all cities, and yet she was languishing for her own kitchen back
home, her own daily round. [...]

It would pass. Mary knew it would pass. The delight in this extraordinary place would return. It was like being seasick for a few days on a ship.

The varporetto was coming. It was a lumbering water-bus, churning up to the Accademia stop and crashing into the floating dock. She waited with the others for the passengers to disembark, then hurried abroad, slid open the door to the seating compartment, and found a place beside a window.

Sitting with her canvas bag between her knees, she extracted her map of the city and decided to get off at the Rialto and followed her nose, obeying her maxim to take pictures of everything. *Push the button, push the button.*

In the meantime there was the whole panorama of the Grand Canal to gawk at, with its changing parade of palaces. Mary glanced back and forth between her map and the view, and held her camera up to the window, taking pictures of one palace after another – Loredan, Rezzonico, Foscari, Papadopoli. Then she transferred her attention to the lively craft on the water – the vaporetti going and coming and the working boats bringing everything necessary for life from the mainland. One carried bottles of *acqua minerale gassata*, another a load of plastic chairs. The men at the tillers hailed each other and raised clenched fists in greeting. *Quick, push the button.* Then she turned her camera lens on a floating pile driver that was smashing thick poles into the water with heavy hammer blows. A red speedboat of the Vigili del Fuoco came along, throwing up a bow wave, and then a blue one of the polizias, roaring by in the other direction.

But it was the gondolas that were the most delectable subjects, as though they had survived from ages past merely to have their pictures taken. Mary could see that they were no good as transporters of human cargo from place to place, certainly not in competition with this clumsy water-bus. You didn't hire a gondola to get somewhere. It was strictly an aesthetic experience.

They were irresistible. Mary took picture after picture through the window of the vaporetto, trying to capture the grace of the gondoliers as they stood in the stern, shifting gently from one foot to the other, rocking slightly forward and back.

She was almost too late to get off at her stop. The Rialto Bridge loomed up before she was ready. The vaporetto was already scraping the floating dock.

Mary jumped out of her seat and crowded forward, just managing to get off before the next crowd of passengers surged on board. [...]

For the rest of the day she wandered without direction, photographing church after church, square after square, rejoicing in side streets where laundry was suspended high overhead, rosy sheets like canopies of heaven, dangling aprons with fluttering strings. When a pulley creaked, she was just in time to catch a hand reaching out to pin a white cloth on the line.

Homesickness was forgotten. Entranced, she drifted north, then west into the *sestiere* of Cannaregio. What was this church? It didn't matter. It was festooned with gesturing sculpture, frenzies of white marble against the sky. *Push the button.* She crossed bridges and found herself in dead ends, then fumbled her way into a broad street full of shoppers. There was a noisy murmur of talk and fragrant whiffs of bread, cigarettes, vanilla, chewing gum. Grapes and pears were arranged in front of a shop like works of art. So were samples of dry pasta in a window – green *tagliatelle agli spinaci*, black *pasta al nero di sepia*, brown *pasta al cacao*.

Heading north again she followed a long *fondamenta* beside the Rio de la Misericordia. By now it was late afternoon, and the tide was rising. Water slopped over the rim of the canal. Mary edged her way along the *fondamenta*, keeping close to the house fronts. When she came to another bridge she crossed it, and found herself in the Ghetto Nuovo, where the pavement was dry.

Yes, of course. This was it, the original ghetto. She had read about the history of the Jews in Venice. It was a long and cruel story. As members of a despised race they had been confined to this little island, an abandoned iron foundry called the Ghetto, and permitted out only at certain hours.

Mary wandered across the square to a wall covered with bronze reliefs, rugged images of cattle cars and crematories. Had Jews been herded into death camps from this city too? Appalled, she murmured it aloud, "Not here too?"

"*Si, si,*" said a voice close behind her.

She turned to see a big man in an old-fashioned black hat. He had a full black beard, crisp and curling. "*Anche qui,*" he said. "Here too."

Mary looked back at the cattle cars, and said simply, "How many? *Quanti?*"

The rabbi frowned, and said nothing for a moment. But he was only translating Italian numbers into English. "Two hundred," he said, and his scowl deepened as he mumbled to himself, "*Quaranta sei.*" Then with a triumphant smile he put it all together. "Two hundred and forty!" Turning away he lifted his hat and added, "Six."

Feebly Mary said, "*Grazie.*" She backed up and lifted her camera and took a picture of the cattle cars.

It was the last shot. The film buzzed backward. She put in new film. She was hungry and exhausted. She wandered across another bridge into the Ghetto Vecchio, took a few more pictures, and gave up. Oh God, it was a long way back!

Beyond the Ghetto Vecchio the water began again. The tide had risen. There was nothing to do but wade. But the main shopping street was dry and full of people coming and going. At San Marcuola Mary boarded a downstream vaporetto and sank into a seat. At once she rummaged in her bag for her notebook and tried to make a list of everything she had seen, all the pictures she had taken.

It was no use. She didn't know where she had been because she had been following her nose, obeying every impulsive whim to go this way rather than that, attracted by the vista from a bridge, or a view of another bridge, or a campanile, or a hand flinging open a shutter. There was no way to make a list. It was all a jumble. [...]

The more Mary went exploring with her camera, the more she was convinced that Venice was the city of Tintoretto. His paintings were everywhere, in church after church – in San Giorgio Maggiore, the Salute, the Frari – and of course in the Ducal Palace, where his *Paradise* was one of the largest paintings in the world.

She was in awe of Tintoretto. One morning, looking for a new route of exploration on her map, she found the words *Casa del Tintoretto* in the middle of Cannaregio.

She had been in this *sestiere* before. She had seen the desiccated body of Santa Lucia of Syracuse in a glass coffin like Snow White's, she had seen the Ghetto Nuovo and the Ghetto Vecchio, she had cashed a traveler's check on the Strada Nuova and stopped at a newsstand for a Paris edition of the *Herald Tribune*.

But she hadn't run across the house of Tintoretto. Everything she had read about him was admirable. Did he live in a palace? Whatever it was, she wanted to find it, to imagine the way he had lived.

It wasn't easy. Cannaregio was a maze of little wandering streets and dead ends. The canal she wanted was the Rio della Sensas. When she found it at last, she was surprised to see a gulf where the water should have been. This part of the rio had been drained. In place of the sparkling jade-green water running so pleasantly in all the other canals, there was only a muddy crevasse.

Crossing the bridge over the empty gully, she looked for the Campo dei Mori. It had to be here somewhere. Yes, of course, here it was, the Square of the Moors. One of them was set into the corner, a clumsy carved figure wearing a kind of turban. Well, fine, but where was Tintoretto's house?

Jane Langton, *The Thief of Venice* (1999)

❊ ❊ ❊

The same advice – simply to wander – comes up in Jeanette Winterson's The Passion.

'This city enfolds upon itself. Canals hide other canals, alleyways cross and criss-cross so that you will not know which is which until you have lived here all your life. Even when you have mastered the squares and you can pass from the Rialto to the Ghetto and out to the lagoon with confidence, there will still be places you can never find and if you do find them you may never see St. Mark's again. Leave plenty of time in your doings and be prepared to go another way, to do something not planned if that is where the streets lead you.'

Jeanette Winterson, *The Passsion* (1987)

❊ ❊ ❊

If you decide to take the 'just wander' advice, it can be useful to understand the way that Venice is divided into a number of distinct districts. Venetian Paolo Barbaro explains – and also treats us to some of the wonderful names of the city's many bridges.

Venice, composed of six sestieri, each of which comprises its own varied quarters, is further divided into *microcittà,* tiny cities or districts – all similar, all completely unique. [...] There's no end to them. It's a continuous aggregate of island-cities, each with its own square, its camp or campiello, its locals engaged on their errands, its rivers of faces and memories, its stores and shops, its church, its old *osteria* or tavern (too often closed these days; whenever it's open, it's a *festa*), its surrounding canal, which defines and limits the island, and its bridges uniting it all to the island beside it.

Sometimes on the far side of a bridge, "any little thing is enough to change it completely," says Martino. When you think about it in terms of *reality*, little or nothing has changed; but your first impression is that it's entirely different, and first impressions are always what count. The lights seem different, as do the canals, the bottlenecks of the calli, the shops, the courtyards and gardens. Often the air, the climate itself, undergoes some large or small transformation. Thus Venice is made up not only of islands, of quarters, districts, sestieri, minicanals and microcities (there are really no names for all these) but also of *aria diversa*: microclimates, distinct enough to recognise as you pass from one to another. [...]

Between Sant'Aponal and the Rialto there's a continuous shifting of types of streets and the names that go with them. This is a small quarter of San Polo devoid of canals, but within a short distance I count twenty different sorts of streets: *calle, calletta, ramo, campo, campiello, salizzada, portico, fondamenta, sottoportico, arco, volto, crosera, riva, ruga, corte, pissina, piscina, pasina ...*

In this "subquarter", as I call it, there are neither canals nor bridges. But as soon as you leave it, the bridges break out all over the place, go wild in every direction. The Crooked Bridge and the Straight Bridge, the Bridge of Swords, the Bridge of the Pots and Pans ... Then there's the Bridge of the Tits and the Bridge of the Melons; the Bridge of Horses, the Bridge of the Madonnas, the Bridge of Lambs and the Bridge of Christs, the Bridges of Ducks, Dyers, and Queens.

As usual, the names of the bridges and streets are rendered in Italian or Venetian seemingly at whim, creating a fantastic, non-stop confusion.

Paolo Barbaro, *Venice Revealed* (1998)
translated by Tami Calliope

* * *

In Penelope Lively's novel, Perfect Happiness, *the protagonist starts off at the most unmissable place of all: Piazza San Marco – St Mark's Square. She opens her map ... but it proves useless and she, too, ends up "simply wandering".*

She went out into the piazza. She passed from the shadow of an arcade into the sun and the heat stunned her. She stood looking around and for an instant, a worrying instant, could not think where she was, why she was there. She could have been dreaming; the buildings, the colonnades, the dome of a church, were like the fantasy landscape of a dream. The moment fled, and she knew again. [...] She was in Venice, and it was mid-afternoon, and she had in her hand a map and a guide-book.

She moved into the shade and looked at the map. She opened the guide-book, and read. [...] She stared at the map, and the geometry of the streets and squares reeled and shimmered. She set off, across open spaces and down alleyway and over bridges. The city ensnared her like a web, a maze. When she tried to match her position to the lines and names on the map there seemed to be no possible relationship. What was, and what was said to be, were not the same. The crumbling fading landscape or arches and pillars and snatches of water and curving bridges and ever-shifting skylines was a stage-set, a tricksy deceptive palimpsest. Alleys furtively opened in walls that appeared blank; streets swung round corners into concealed squares; canals blocked her passage. She abandoned the map and simply wandered, digested by the city.

Penelope Lively, *Perfect Happiness* (1983)

* * *

The problem for American writer Mary McCarthy is that there seems to be no difference between 'tourist Venice' and 'real Venice'. Everything is so well-known

*– the buildings, the traditions, the history, the famous
visitors, the artists – that the city seems to be a postcard of itself.*

Attila opened the story; refugees fleeing from him on the mainland sought safety on the fishing islets and began to build their
improbable city, houses of wattles and twigs set on piles driven
into the mud – "like sea birds' nests," wrote Cassiodorus, secre-
tary of Theodoric, "half on sea and half on land and spread
like the Cyclades over the surface of the waters." Napoleon
finished the story, as he closed in the Piazza San Marco with
the Fabbrica Nuova at the west end, giving each – square and
narrative – its final, necessary form. [...]

And it was thanks to Napoleon that on the plebeian level
a gondolier had the final word. Examining Napoleon's illus-
trated proclamation, which showed the armorial lion of St
Mark's holding the Book, in which the old inscription, *"Pax
tibi, Marce, Evangelisto meus,"* was replaced by the new Word
of the day, "The Rights of Men and Citizens," the gondolier is
supposed to have commented, "At last he's turned the page."

But from Napoleon's point of view, surely, this was just
the trouble with Venice – the increment of childish history, of
twice-told tales. The ducal bonnet, the Inquisitors, the Bocca
del Leone, into which anonymous denunciations were slipped,
the Doge's golden umbrella, the Bucintoro, the Marriage of the
Adriatic, the Ring, the Bridge of Sighs, Casanova, the Leads,
Shylock, the Rialto, Titian, Tintoretto, *les dames de Venise.*
The Capture of the body of St Mark, Lepanto, the pigeons,
the pirates and the brides, the Taking of Constantinople, with
the blind, fearless old Doge Dandolo leading the attack, Marco
Polo, the Queen of Cyprus, and (still yet to come, but already,
so to speak, on the agenda) Byron on the Lido on Horseback,
Byron swimming the Grand Canal, "Julian and Madolo,"
Byron in the Armenian convent, Wagner in the Piazza listening

to "Tannhäuser" played by the Austrian band, Wagner in the Palazzo Vendramin, Browning, D'Annunzio, Duse, and, finally, last and first, the gondola, the eternal gondola, with its steel prow and its witty gondolier, to a "new man", a leveller, what insufferable tedium, what a stagnant canal stench must have emanated from all this! [...] When Napoleon announced he would be an Attila, his irritation cannot have been purely political; it must have been an impatience not so much with an obsolete, reactionary form of government – not so much even with the past (he was awed by the Sphinx and the Pyramids) – as with an eternal present, with a city that had become a series of souvenirs and "views". [...]

Ant there's no pretending that the tourist Venice is not the real Venice, which is possible with other cities – Rome and Florence and Naples. The tourist Venice *is* Venice: the gondolas, the sunsets, the changing light, Florian's, Quadri's, Torcello, Harry's Bar, Murano, Burano, the pigeons, the glass beads, the *vaporetto*. Venice is a folding picture postcard of itself.

Mary McCarthy, *Venice Observed* (1956)

✽ ✽ ✽

When Colin and Mary, in Ian McEwan's The Comfort of Strangers, *arrive in the city, their first experience of St. Mark's Square is less positive than it might be ...*

To reach the hotel, it was necessary to walk across one of the great tourist attractions of the world, an immense wedge-shaped expanse of paving, enclosed on three sides by dignified arcaded buildings and dominated at its open end by a redbrick clock tower, and beyond that a celebrated cathedral of white domes and glittering façade, a triumphant accretion, so it had often been described, of many centuries of civilization. Assembled on the two longer sides of the square, facing across the paving stones like opposing armies, were the tightly packed

ranks of chairs and round tables belonging to the long established cafés; adjacent orchestras, staffed and conducted by men
in dinner jackets, oblivious to the morning heat, played simultaneously martial and romantic music, waltzes and extracts
from popular operas with thunderous climaxes. Everywhere
pigeons banked, strutted and excreted, and each café orchestra
paused uncertainly after the earnest, puny applause of its
nearest customers. Tourists surged across the brilliantly-lit
open ground, or wheeled off in small groups and dissolved into
the monochrome patchwork of light and shade within the delicately colonnaded arcades. Two-thirds, perhaps, of the adult
males carried cameras.

Colin and Mary had walked with difficulty from the boat
and now, before crossing the square, stood in the diminishing
shade of the clock tower. Mary took a succession of deep
breaths, and over the din suggested that they find a drink of
water here. Keeping close together, they set off round the edge
of the square, but there were no vacant tables, there were no
tables even that could be shared, and it became apparent that
much of the movement backwards and forwards across the
square consisted of people in search of a place to sit down,
and that those who left for the labyrinthine streets did so in
exasperation.

Finally, and only by standing several minutes at the table
of an elderly couple who writhed in their seats waving their
bill, they were able to sit, and then it was obvious that the
table was on a remote flank of their waiter's territory, and that
many others who craned their necks and snapped their fingers
unheard would receive attention before them. [...]

The two orchestras had stopped at once, and the players
were making their way towards the arcades, to the bars of their
respective cafés; without their music, the square seemed even
more spacious, only partially filled by the sounds of footsteps,
the sharp click of smart shoes, the slap of sandals; and voices,

murmurs of awe, children's shouts, parental commands of restraint. Mary folded her arms and let her head drop.

Colin stood up and waved both arms at a waiter who nodded and began to move towards them, collecting orders and empty glasses as he came. 'I can't believe it,' Colin cried exultantly.

'We should have brought them with us,' Mary said to her lap.

Colin was still on his feet. 'He's actually coming!' He sat down and tugged at her wrist. 'What would you like?'

'It was mean of us to leave them behind.'

'I think it was rather considerate.'

The waiter, a large, affluent-looking man with a thick, greying beard and gold-rimmed glasses, was suddenly at their table inclining towards them, eyebrows slightly cocked.

'What do you want, Mary?' Colin whispered urgently.

Mary folded her hands in her lap and said, 'A glass of water, without ice.'

'Yes, *two* of those,' Colin said eagerly, 'and ... '

The waiter straightened and a short hiss escaped his nostrils. 'Water?' he said distantly. His eyes moved between them, appraising their dishevelment. He took a step backwards and nodded towards a corner of the square. 'Is a tap.'

As he began to move away, Colin span round in his chair and caught his sleeve. 'No, but waiter,' he pleaded. 'We also wanted some coffee and some ... '

The waiter shook his arm free. 'Coffee!' he repeated, his nostrils flared in derision. 'Two coffee?'

'Yes, yes!'

The man shook his head and was gone.

Colin slumped in his chair, closed his eyes and shook his head slowly; Mary struggled to sit up straight.

She kicked his foot gently under the table. 'Come on. It's only ten minutes to the hotel.' Colin nodded but he did not open his eyes. 'We can have a shower, and sit on our balcony and have anything we want brought up to us.' As Colin's chin sank towards his chest, so Mary became more animated. 'We can get into bed. Mmm, those clean white sheets. We'll close the shutters. Can you imagine anything better? We can … '

'All right,' Colin said dully. 'Let's walk to the hotel.' But neither of them stirred.

Mary pursed her lips, and then said, 'He's probably bringing the coffee anyway. When people shake their heads, here, it can mean all sorts of things.'

As the morning heat had intensified, the crowds had diminished; there were now sufficient tables, and those who still walked in the square were dedicated sightseers, or citizens with real destinations, all scattered figures who, dwarfed by the immensity of vacant space, shimmered in the warped air. Across the square the orchestra had reassembled and was beginning a Viennese waltz.

Ian McEwan, *The Comfort of Strangers* (1981)

* * *

In his short story 'Crooner', Kazuo Ishiguro introduces the musicians who play for the tourists in St Mark's Square and help to give it the atmosphere for which it is famous.

The morning I spotted Tony Gardner sitting among the tourists, spring was just arriving here in Venice. We'd completed our first full week outside in the piazza – a relief, let me tell you, after all those stuffy hours performing from the back of the café, getting in the way of customers wanting to use the staircase. There was quite a breeze that morning, and our brand-new marquee was flapping all around us, but we were all feeling a little bit brighter and fresher, and I guess it showed in our music.

But here I am talking like I'm a regular band member. Actually, I'm one of the 'gypsies', as the other musicians call us, one

of the guys who move around the piazza, helping out whichever of the three café orchestras needs us. Mostly I play here
at the Caffè Lavena, but on a busy afternoon, I might do a set
with the Quadri boys, go over to the Florian, then back across
the square to the Lavena. I get on fine with them all – and
with the waiters too – and in any other city I'd have a regular
position by now. But in this place, so obsessed with tradition
and the past, everything's upside down. Anywhere else, being
a guitar player would go in a guy's favour. But here? A guitar!
The café managers get uneasy. It looks too modern, the tourists won't like it. Last autumn I got myself a vintage jazz model
with an oval sound-hole, the kind of thing Django Reinhardt
might have played, so there was no way anyone would mistake
me for a rock-and-roller. That made things a little easier, but
the café managers, they still don't like it. The truth is, if you're
a guitarist, you can be Joe Pass, they still wouldn't give you a
regular job in this square.

There's also, of course, the small matter of my not being
Italian, never mind Venetian. It's the same for that big Czech
guy with the alto sax. We're well liked, we're needed by the
other musicians, but we don't quite fit the official bill. Just
play and keep your mouth shut, that's what the café managers
always say. That way the tourists won't know you're not
Italian. Wear your suit, sunglasses, keep the hair combed back,
no one will know the difference, just don't start talking.

But I don't do too bad. All three café orchestras, especially
when they have to play at the same time from their rival tents,
they need a guitar – something soft, solid, but amplified,
thumping out the chords from the back. I guess you're thinking,
three bands playing at the same time in the same square, that
would sound like a real mess. But the Piazza San Marco's big
enough to take it. A tourist strolling across the square will hear
one tune fade out, another fade in, like he's shifting the dial on
a radio. What tourists can't take too much of is the classical

stuff, all these instrumental versions of famous arias. Okay, this is San Marco, they don't want the latest pop hit. But every few minutes they want something they recognise, maybe an old Julie Andrews number, or the theme from a famous movie. I remember once last summer, going from band to band and playing "The Godfather" nine times in one afternoon.

Anyway there we were that spring morning, playing in front of a good crowd of tourists, when I saw Tony Gardner, sitting alone with his coffee, almost directly in front of us, maybe six metres back from our marquee. We get famous people in the square all the time, we never make a fuss. At the end of a number, maybe a quiet word will go around the band members. Look, there's Warren Beatty. Look, it's Kissinger. That woman, she's the one who was in the movie about the men who swap their faces. We're used to it. This is the Piazza San Marco after all. But when I realised it was Tony Gardner sitting there, that was different. I *did* get excited.

Kazuo Ishiguro, "Crooner" from Nocturnes (2009)

❉ ❉ ❉

The three oldest and most venerable cafés on St Mark's Square are the Lavena (much loved by Wagner), the Quadri (a favourite with Austrians in the nineteenth century) and, the most famous of all, the Florian, haunt of many celebrities both past and present. Writer and poet Henri de Régnier (1864–1936) captures something of its atmosphere.

As you know, the café Florian is made up of several adjoining rooms, decorated in various styles and having the atmosphere of private lounges. Among these is one for which I had a particular affection. Its walls were adorned with mirrors and frescoes under glass to protect them from smoke and general damage. These frescoes depicted figures dressed in the costumes of various nationalities. Two of them, in particular, amused me: a Turk in a turban and a Chinaman with a pigtail. It was beneath the Chinese gentleman that I most often chose to sit, upon the divans upholstered in red velvet, in front of one of those round marble tables the top of which turns upon the single leg supporting it. My favourite place had just become free as I entered the almost empty room. At the other end of it, two Venetians were holding forth while finishing off their glass of water, and, in one corner, an old man with a red nose swigged down the last drops of a little glass of *strega*. I ordered a glass of punch from the waiter. Before he brought it, the two people who'd been talking got up and left. The man with the red nose waved to them. However, the waiter wasn't long bringing the punch I'd ordered. It was a pinkish drink at once fragrant and delicate in flavour. Slowly I drank a few mouthfuls: my negative mood dissolved and changed to a feeling of well-being. That sense of relaxation was most welcome. I had definitely done the right thing coming to the dear old Florian, where I had formerly spent so many evenings, and sitting beneath the Chinaman. I turned a little towards the figure in the fresco. The Chinaman looked at me with a mocking bonhomie and seemed to be congratulating me for having visited him before returning to the hotel ...

Henri de Régnier, *L'Entrevue* (1919)
translated by E. F. Morgan

✳ ✳ ✳

Saint Mark's Square – possibly the most visited, photographed, and described square in the world: traditionally 'the drawing-room of Europe' ... though there seems some doubt as to whether it was Napoleon or French poet Alfred de Musset who first called it that. Henry James and L. P. Hartley give a little more of the atmosphere.

Piazza San Marco, always, as a great social saloon, a smooth-floored, blue-roofed chamber of amenity, favourable to talk; or rather, to be exact, not in the middle, but at the point where our pair had paused by a common impulse after leaving the great mosque-like church. It rose now, domed and pinnacled, but a little way behind them, and they had in front the vast empty space, enclosed by its arcades, to which at that hour movement and traffic were mostly confined. Venice was at breakfast.

Henry James, *The Wings of the Dove* (1902)

❉ ❉ ❉

Lady Nelly came out from the cool, porphyry-tinted twilight of St Mark's into the strong white sunshine of the Piazza.

The heat, like a lover, had possessed the day; its presence, as positive and self-confident as an Italian tenor's, rifled the senses and would not be denied. Lady Nelly moved on into the glare; she wore dark glasses to shield her eyes, and her face looked pale under her broad-brimmed hat, for the fashion for being sunburnt was one she did not follow. A true Venetian, she did not try to avoid treading on the pigeons, which nodded to each other as they bustled about her feet; but when she came in line with the three flag-poles she paused and looked around her.

The scene was too familiar for her to take in its detail, though as always she felt unconsciously uplifted by it. The drawing-room of Europe, Henry James had called it, and as befitted a drawing-room, it was well furnished with chairs. Those on the right, belonging to the cafés of Lavena and the Quadri, and enjoying the full sunlight, were already well patronised; even to her darkened vision the white coats of the waiters flashing to and fro looked blindingly bright. But at Florian's, on the left, where the shadow fell on all but the outermost tiers of tables, hardly anyone was sitting, and the waiters stood like a group of statues, mutely contemplating their lack of custom.

Indescribably loud, the report of the midday gun startled Lady Nelly from her meditation. The pigeons launched themselves into the air as though the phenomenon was new to them; the loiterers checked their watches or stared into the sky; there was a general feeling of détente, as if a crisis had been passed and nerves could relax for another twenty-four hours.

To Lady Nelly it was now clear that she wanted to go to Florian's. As she bent her steps that way, the waiters sighted her from afar, and began to talk among themselves as though speculating which of them would have the pleasure of serving her. Each had his province beyond whose bounds he might not pass. This Lady Nelly knew well, and she had her favourite, though she made her arrival in his domain seem quite accidental. With a smile that seemed to circle the top of his bald head he came out to meet her and held the chair for her, as she sat down.

L.P. Hartley, *Eustace and Hilda* (1958)

❊ ❊ ❊

In these two extracts from her novel Miss Garnet's Angel, *Sally Vickers first takes Miss Garnet on a walk to San Marco, arriving at the square in the late afternoon and visiting the Basilica, then makes her climb up to the famous horses on the roof.*

Miss Garnet had chosen one of the further reaches of the almost-island-which-is-Venice to stay in and from this remoter quarter the walk to the Piazza San Marco takes time. Despite Signora Mignelli's instructions Miss Garnet did not yet feel equal to experimenting with the *vaporetti* and besides, exercise, she felt, was what was called for. She walked purposefully along the narrow *calle* which led down to the Accademia (where, the Reverend Crystal promised, a wealth of artistic treasure awaited her). At the wooden Accademia bridge she halted. Ahead of her, like a vast soap bubble formed out of the circling, dove-coloured mists, stood Santa Maria della Salute, the church which breasts the entrance to Venice's Grand Canal.

'Oh!' cried Miss Garnet. She caught at her throat and then at Harriet's veil, scrabbling it back from her eyes to see more clearly. And oh, the light! 'Lord, Lord,' sighed Julia Garnet.

She did not know why she had used those words as she moved off, frightened to stay longer lest the unfamiliar beauty so captivate her that she turn to stone, as she later amusingly phrased it to herself. But it was true it was a kind of fear she felt, almost as if she was fleeing some harrowing spectre who stalked her progress. Across another *campo*, then over bridges, along further alleys, past astonishing pastries piled high in gleaming windows, past shops filled with bottled liquor, alarming knives, swathes of patterned paper. Once she passed an artists' suppliers where, in spite of the spectre, she stopped to admire the window packed with square dishes heaped with brilliant coloured powders: *oro, oro pallido, argento, lacca rossa* – gold, silver, red, the colours of alchemy, thought Miss Garnet, hurrying on, for she had read about alchemy when she was teaching the Renaissance to the fifth form.

At the edge of the Piazza she halted. Let the spectre do its worst, for here was the culmination of her quest. Before her stood the campanile, the tall bell-tower, and behind it, in glimmering heaps and folds, in gilded wings and waved encrustations, emerged the outline of St Mark's. People might speak of St Mark's as a kind of dream but Miss Garnet had never known such dreams. Once, as a child, she dreamed she had become a mermaid; that was the closest she had ever come to this.

Measuring each step she walked across the Piazza. Although still afternoon the sky was beginning to darken and already a pearl fingernail clipping of moon was appearing, like an inspired throwaway gesture designed to point up the whole effect of the basilica's sheen. Reaching the arched portals Miss Garnet stopped, wondering if it was all right to go on. But it must be, look there were other tourists – how silly she was, of course one didn't have to be a Christian to enter and inspect a renowned example of Byzantine architecture.

Inside the great cathedral before her a line of people shuffled forward. Above her, and on all sides, light played and danced

70

from a million tiny surfaces of refracted gold. A dull smell of onions disconcertingly filled her nostrils. What was it? Years of sweat, perhaps, perfuming the much-visited old air. [...]

Silver lamps burned dimly in the recesses. Above her and on all sides loomed strange glittering mosaic figures, in a background of unremitting gold. A succession of images – lions, lambs, flowers, thorns, eagles, serpents, dragons, doves – wove before her startled eyes a shimmering vision, awful and benign. Like blood forcing a route through long-constricted arteries a kind of wild rejoicing began to cascade through her. Stumbling slightly she made her way to a seat on the main aisle. [...]

A notice reminded her that in all this she had never yet climbed up to see the famous bronze horses. It was bound to be crowded inside the basilica. And she was curious to look down on the Piazza from the vantage point above. She set off up steep stone stairs.

Coming out into the upper gallery she saw a body hanging from a tree. Judas Iscariot: the traitor. The mosaicist must have put him up here, away out of sight. Poor Judas! How must it have felt, betraying what you knew to be the best? Maybe that was the job of Saraqûel, the fifth angel? To defend us against self-treachery?

But the horses? She had come to see the horses. It was said they were no longer safe to stand outside where the polluted air might ransack their gilded bronze sides. She had seen one of them once when, dutifully, she had queued in a line at the British Museum. But she had no proper memory of it.

She made her way along the finger-smoothed marble and suddenly, she caught her breath for there, like ancient gods, they were, ears pricked, nostrils flared, each with a hoof delicately raised. Thousands of years old, they had survived magisterially their history as loot and plunder. Whatever were such riches doing in this poky room? Who cared about the pollution? They should surely be outside in the free air! Horses are like dogs, she reflected, hurrying from the room: guardians of our instincts.

Julia went out and onto the roof. It was early evening and down below, with the heat beginning to abate, tourists had begun to fill the Piazza. On the sloping marble surfaces she walked past the replica horses, reaching up to touch one on the hoof. Tough always to be the substitute! She sat down at the corner, feeling the bulk of the basilica at her back, on a level with the blue and gilded clock-tower which strikes with hammers the quarters of each hour for the city of Venice.

Sally Vickers, *Miss Garnet's Angel* (2000)

❋ ❋ ❋

Another visit to San Marco and a view of those iconic horses ...

I found myself at one end of the Rialto, the hooded bridge still curling into darkness, the rubbish floating and unfurling in the low unearthly wind which troubles those few inches just above the earth at dawn, and felt, instead of saw, a lightness coming in the sky; and I began to run, as I had not in years, without a thought in mind, alive and shaking weariness away, ran filled with simple pleasure at the coming dawn and living, running with youth out into a future I could not and would not ever understand. The few sad figures shifting out to work ignored me; for them the dawn was silence filled with knowledge of a day alive with heat and labour, but I knew only where my feet were leading, ducking and weaving and turning, turning always to face that glimmer, turning to meet the dawn until at last, before I had expected it, breathless, surprised at my surprise, I stood there where an empty mind had led me, before San Marco, in the place of dreams.

The Piazza still stood darkened. The light now showed through half the eastern sky as though a silk lay over it, and it was time before I realised that light would come before the dawn, because the basilica stood before the rising sun which would illuminate the sky before it rose above the swooping oriental rooftops of the church. I waited, not knowing what to expect. The glad battalions of pigeons had begun to stir, but idly, lifting and swaying, well aware that only day would bring the people out and the first prospects of a meal. In the colonnades on either side of me sweepers were shifting the litter from place to place, heedless of one mad Englishman up to see a time of day when proper visitors and people with their senses still about them still lay safe abed. The only excuse for early rising is work, except when we are young, or old, when fear of time and death makes night a torment and every further waking hour an agonising gift.

The light seeped slowly westward until the sky was one blue haze, the tender moment of the day when all the world seems perfect however terrible we know it all to be. Then at last the sky behind San Marco began to whiten, the way that skin does when you press it, and more than any church I had ever seen the basilica seemed built for display, the final vista of a square built as a stage set to show off the power of an empire long since vanished. I was too young to wonder then how later ages glory in those monuments the past leaves for them which had been most extravagant when the past was now, and monuments meant taxes and bankrupt treasuries.

Then I saw them, smaller than I had expected, against that wild, extravagant façade – four horses cast in bronze when God and the world were young, brought westward stage by stage by conqueror after conqueror, until at last they rested here as emblems of the city's wide dominion over all the waters of the east of the Middle Sea, waters which bore the traffic of the East to Europe for longer years than we remember, traffic which had drawn these horses with it, as they seemed now to draw the sun.

I had not realised, and no one had warned me (for who goes seeing sights at dawn?), how cunningly down the years the grand and terrible old men who governed the One Republic had created the eastern, unapologetic church which was the emblem of their state, trading from early years with Antioch, Ephesus, all of Asia, and Jerusalem, owing no dominion to the mighty tyranny of Rome; for here in the building which contained a slab on which was carved, in medieval Latin, the city's proudest boast – 'Here lies the body of Mark, the Evangelist' (and where, the city fathers asked, in Rome could anyone show you Peter?) – they had produced a ship, an argosy, its domes the bulging sails, to accompany each dawn, in silent confidence, the rising sun, the guarantor of gold.

It was day, and light caught all the gilded, coppered, brazen surfaces of the basilica, till they were also fire, and black against them stood four horses. They are not grand, those horses. They do not rear in fierce exultation. They were cast by an early technology, standing three-square on the ground with one foreleg raised, and in the mad riot of that spectacle at dawn it is their easiness, their small dark simplicity, which makes the eyes turn away from all their cloud of witness of fire and light, and see them for what they are, the oldest things of man in that old city, five thousand years and more some say, cast far to the East in the early youth of man, and say, as I said then, not knowing what I meant (I still do not, although I know that what I said was, in some extraordinary way, the simple truth), 'These are the Horses of the Sun'.

H.S. Bhabra, *Gestures* (1986)

✳ ✳ ✳

Rumer Godden's Pippa braves the throngs of tourists in Saint Mark's Basilica.

She pushed through the crowd to go into the Basilica. […]
    She found herself propelled by the press of people to go around the Pala d'Oro, the famous screen of gold with its

panels of jewels that stood behind the high altar. The floor was uneven; under the moving feet she saw patterns. There was the smell of warm bodies, of the slight dampness of stone and marble, a scent of incense – a fair haze of it hung in the air high above. The tourists were a little hushed, though there was a continuous clicking of cameras and the loud voices of guides informing their groups. They shouldn't do that in here, Pippa thought, though why she minded she did not know. She had never heard the word sanctity.

As she extricated herself from the queue and looked round, she had the impression of dim spaces, side chapels with altars, pillars and galleries, all with carved figures and gleams of gold, but she was not looking at the Basilica and its treasures, she was watching the people.

There were some who did not stare and look but went at once to kneel and pray; some seemed to be in groups – she saw a bevy of Japanese. They must be pilgrims, she guessed. There were, too, women old and young, obviously locals, who flumped their full baskets and plastic bags down, knelt and prayed. Some of the younger ones had children, probably fetched from school – Venetian children all seemed to be well dressed. A few of them were allowed to light candles.

Now that her eyes had grown accustomed, she saw the great church was alive with glinting light, a flickering of candles beside the altars of some of the chapels – only the sanctuary lamp on its jewelled holder beside the high altar was steady. The Basilica was, too, full of murmurings, people were praying by the candlestands and she watched as coins and small notes were dropped into the money boxes; then hands held the taper, lit from another candle; for a moment faces were illuminated, often the lips moving in prayer.

Rumer Godden, Pippa Passes (1994)

✳ ✳ ✳

And right next to St Mark's is the Doges' (or Ducal) Palace. Charles Dickens gives a description of it that is both dream-like and persistently real.

I came upon a place of such surpassing beauty, and such grandeur, that all the rest was poor and faded, in comparison with its absorbing loveliness.

It was a great piazza, as I thought, anchored, like all the rest, in the deep ocean. On its broad bosom was a palace, more majestic and magnificent in its old age than all the buildings of the earth in the high prime and fullness of their youth. Cloisters and galleries – so light, they might have been the work of fairy hands, so strong that centuries had battered them in vain – wound round and round this palace, and enfolded it with a cathedral, gorgeous in the wild, luxuriant fancies of the East. At no great distance from its porch, a lofty tower, standing by itself and rearing its proud head, alone, into the sky, looked out upon the Adriatic Sea. Near to the margin of the stream were two ill-omened pillars of red granite, one having on its top a figure with a sword and shield, the other a winged lion. Not far from these again, a second tower, richest of the rich in all its decorations, even here where all was rich, sustained aloft a great orb gleaming with gold and deepest blue, the Twelve Signs painted on it, and a mimic sun revolving in its course around them, while above, two bronze giants hammered out the hours upon a sounding bell. An oblong square of lofty houses of the whitest stone, surrounded by a light and beautiful arcade, formed part of this enchanted scene; and, here and there, gay masts for flags rose, tapering, from the pavement of the unsubstantial ground. I thought I entered the Cathedral and went in and out among its many arches, traversing its whole extent. A grand and dreamy structure of immense proportions, golden with old mosaics, redolent of perfumes, dim with the smoke of incense, costly in treasure of precious stones and metals, glittering through iron bars, holy with the bodies of deceased saints, rainbow-hued with windows of stained glass, dark with carved woods and coloured marbles, obscure in its vast heights and lengthened distances; shining with silver lamps and winking lights, unreal, fantastic, solemn, inconceivable throughout.

I thought I entered the old palace, pacing silent galleries and council-chambers, where the old rulers of this mistress of the waters looked sternly out, in pictures, from the walls, and where her high-prowed galleys, still victorious on canvas, fought and conquered as of old. I thought I wandered through its halls of state and triumph – bare and empty now! – and musing on its pride and might, extinct, for that was past, all past. I heard a voice say, 'Some tokens of its ancient rule and some consoling reasons for its downfall may be traced here yet!'

I dreamed that I was led on, then, into some jealous rooms, communicating with a prison near the palace, separated from it by a lofty bridge crossing a narrow street and called, I dreamed, The Bridge of Sighs.

But first I passed two jagged slits in a stone wall, the lions' mouths – now toothless – where, in the distempered horror of my sleep, I thought denunciations of innocent men to the old wicked Council had been dropped through, many a time, when the night was dark. So, when I saw the council-room to which prisoners were taken for examination, and the door by which they passed out when they were condemned – a door that never closed upon a man with life and hope before him – my heart appeared to die within me.

It was smitten harder though, when, torch in hand, I descended from the cheerful day into two ranges, one below another, of dismal, awful, horrible stone cells. They were quite dark. Each had a loop-hole in its massive wall, where, in the old time, every day a torch was placed – I dreamed – to light the prisoner within, for half an hour. The captives, by the glimmering of these brief rays, had scratched and cut inscriptions in the blackened vaults. I saw them. For their labour with a rusty nail's point had outlived their agony and them, through many generations.

One cell, I saw, in which no man remained for more than four-and-twenty hours, being marked for dead before he entered it. Hard by, another, and a dismal one whereto, at midnight, the confessor came – a monk brown-robed and hooded – ghastly in the day and free bright air, but in the midnight of that murky prison, Hope's extinguisher and Murder's herald. I had my foot upon the spot where, at the same dread hour, the shriven prisoner was strangled, and struck my hand upon the guilty door – low-browed and stealthy – through which the lumpish sack was carried out into a boat and rowed away and drowned where it was death to cast a net.

Charles Dickens, 'An Italian Dream' in *Pictures from Italy* (1846)

✺ ✺ ✺

Henry James advises trying to see the Palace when there are fewer tourists about ... and, unlike Dickens, avoids dwelling on its darker history.

This deeply original building is of course the loveliest thing in Venice, and a morning's stroll there is a wonderful illumination. Cunningly select your hour – half the enjoyment of Venice is a question of dodging – and enter at about one o'clock, when the tourists have flocked off to lunch and the echoes of the charming chambers have gone to sleep among the sunbeams. There is no brighter place in Venice – by which I mean that on the whole there is none half so bright. The reflected sunshine plays up through the great windows from the glittering lagoon and shimmers and twinkles over gilded walls and ceilings. All the history of Venice, all its splendid stately past, glows around you in a strong sealight. Everyone here is magnificent, but the great Veronese is the most magnificent of all. He swims before you in a silver cloud; he thrones in an eternal morning. The deep blue sky burns behind him, streaked across with milky bars; the white colonnades sustain the richest canopies, under which the first gentlemen and ladies in the world both render homage and receive it. Their glorious garments rustle in the air of the sea and their sun-lighted faces are the very complexion of Venice. The mixture of pride and piety, of politics and religion, of art and patriotism, gives a splendid dignity to every scene.

Henry James, *Italian Hours* (1909)

❖ ❖ ❖

After the Bridge of Sighs, the most famous bridge in Venice is the Rialto.

We cross the famous Rialto Bridge, going up the middle between all the shops, which are tiny alcoves stuffed full like treasure chests, selling watches, jewels, leather, cashmere. People crowd the edges, staring down mesmerised. Here in the centre of the city, pinned over the Canal Grande, everything seems to be half bright air, half jewelled water – and all money.

Bidisha, *Venetian Masters* (2008)

❖ ❖ ❖

The Bridge of the Rialto is a name to conjure with, but, honestly speaking, it is scarcely the gem of the composition. There are of course two ways of taking it – from the water or from the upper passage, where its small shops and booths abound in Venetian character; but it mainly counts as a feature of the Canal when seen from the gondola or even from the awful *vaporetto*. The great curve of its single arch is much to be commended, especially when, coming from the direction of the railway-station, you see it frame with its sharp compass-line the perfect picture, the reach of the Canal on the other side. But the backs of the little shops make from the water a graceless collective hump, and the inside view is the diverting one.

Henry James, *Italian Hours* (1909)

* * *

A long, narrow island in the south of Venice, Giudecca has long been a culturally distinct part of the city. Its monasteries used to give sanctuary to fugitives – including Michelangelo (banished from Florence in 1529). During the 18th century, the scandalous parties held in the island's beautiful gardens gained the district a reputation for drunken orgies. By the late nineteenth and early twentieth centuries, however, the monasteries and gardens had given way to factories, workshops, and tightly-packed housing. But one of the island's glories is the church of Il Redentore (The Most Holy Redeemer) in which one can find paintings by Veronese and Tintoretto, among others. Well worth a visit. Here are three pieces on the district by very different writers.

Whatever else it might be, the Giudecca is a now-bucolic spit of land, three hundred yards across the Giudecca Canal from the heart of Venice. It has one important church, no major tourist attractions, and no tourist shops. It was the site of the last real factories in Venice and has thus been associated with a somewhat different, rougher working class than elsewhere in the city. People who live on Giudecca consider themselves a breed apart, which, in one way or another, is how residents of all the islands in the lagoon feel about themselves.

John Berendt, *City of Falling Angels* (2005)

* * *

The island of Giudecca was a part of Venice Brunetti seldom visited. Visible from Piazza San Marco, visible, in fact, from the entire flank of the island, in places no more than a hundred metres away, it nevertheless lived in strange isolation from the rest of the city. The grisly stories that appeared in the paper with embarrassing frequency, of children bitten by rats or people found dead of overdoses, always seemed to take place on the Giudecca. Even the presence of a dethroned monarch and a fading movie star of the fifties couldn't redeem it in the popular consciousness as a sinister, backward place where nasty things happened.

Brunetti, along with a large part of the city, usually went there in July, during the Feast of the Redeemer, which celebrated the cessation of the plague of 1576. For two days, a pontoon bridge joined the Giudecca with the main island, allowing the faithful to walk across the water to the Church of the Redeemer, there to give thanks for yet another instance of the divine intervention that seemed so frequently to have saved or spared the city.

Donna Leon, *Death at La Fenice* (1992)

✳ ✳ ✳

The quarter-moon was resting on the roofs of the palaces as they came out into the Grand Canal. The shadows stretching half-way across divided the canal, almost theatrically, into a light area and a dark one, so that there seemed to be two processions going side by side; one a string of lanterns with black shapes following them, the other brilliantly lit, the details of each boat distinctly visible, though the lamps they carried were pale and feeble. But the noise on both sides was the same, laughter and singing and festive shouts, and the plangent thrum of mandolines – a heady, expectant sound. [...]

They turned to the right into the moonless darkness of a side canal. Here the traffic was so thick around them that they could almost hear their neighbours breathe; and Silvestro, disregarding professional etiquette, kept bending down to fend them off with his hand. To accept the pace of the crowd and drift with it was abhorrent to him. A few minutes of this awkward bumpy progress brought them to a bridge. They passed under and were out on the broad water of the Giudecca Canal.

Here, though they themselves were still in shadow, they had the moonlight again; the great expanse of water was dotted with boats to its farther shore, and as they went on the boats grew thicker. Many were lashed together. A man with a flagon in his hand leaned over and filled a glass in his neighbour's boat. The men flitted like shadows between the pale dresses of the women. They moved about, the women sat still; Eustace had glimpses of copper-coloured faces, each the fragment of a smile.

Hugging the bank, Silvestro pressed on. His purposefulness contrasted with the carefree mood of the revellers round him, yet somehow enhanced it. All along the fondamenta boats were moored, and as they drew nearer to the bridge Eustace saw that every available roadstead had been taken. Where would they go? Suddenly there was a seething of waters, and the gondola, pulled back on its haunches, stopped in the middle of its private storm. An urgent whisper from Silvestro and the boat on their left loosened itself from a post and slid away into the darkness. Silvestro manoeuvred the gondola into its place. [...]

The place was indeed well chosen, and Silvestro had disposed the gondola so that the reclining ladies and their upright escorts opposite had only to turn their heads to see the church of the Redentore. Silvery and expectant, looking larger than by day, it met them almost full-face. Behind them the moon sent a track across the water which, continually broken by the dark forms of boats, made nevertheless a ribbon of light between them and the church where it gloriously terminated; and on their left the bridge, which had also gained in impressiveness since the morning, made an angle with the line of moonlight, a slender black-and-white V whose apex was the church. In both directions people were crowding across the bridge. Eustace could hear their voices and the shuffle of their feet, and see them descend, slow-moving and tiny, on to the space in front of the great church. Up the steps they went until the shadow of the high doorway, thrown inwards, effaced them as they crossed the threshold.

Beyond the noise of voices, the snatches of music, the swinging of paper lanterns, the tilting and dipping of sterns and bows, the church in its grey immensity stood motionless and silent. Now that Eustace was growing accustomed to the light he saw that the façade was faintly flood-lit by the lamps at its base, a wash of gold had crept along the silver. Yet how stern were the uncompromising straight lines, drawn like a diagram against the night; how intimidating the shadows behind the buttresses which supported roof and dome. The church drew his eyes to it with a promise which was almost threatening, so powerfully did it affect his mind.

They had finished supper, they had eaten the duck, the mulberries and the mandarins, the traditional fare of the feast, and were sitting with their champagne glasses in front of them on the white tablecloth when the first rocket went up. Eustace heard the swish like the hissing intake of a giant breath, and his startled nerves seemed to follow its flight. Then with a soft round plop the knot of tension broke, and the core of fiery green dissolved into single stars which floated down with infinite languor towards the thousands of upturned faces. A ripple of delight went through the argosy of pleasure-seekers.

L. P. Hartley, *Eustace and Hilda* (1958)

❋ ❋ ❋

Just off the eastern tip of Giudecca is the island of San Giorgio with its famous Palladian church. In this little gem from Stone Virgin, *Barry Unsworth describes the view in two contrasting lights. (And it's another church to put on the itinerary.)*

They were on the Riva degli Schiavoni, looking across to the marvellously fabricated shape of San Giorgio with its line of little boats along the front, like beading. Earlier, when he had been on his way to meet Wiseman, there had been a powdering of mist in the air, thicker on the broader water where the Giudecca Canal opened into the basin of San Marco, obscuring the lines of the church, softening the outline of dome and campanile. Now, something like two hours later, the light was clear and sparkling on the water, every detail of Palladio's design was radiantly distinct, the whole thing, church and island together, seemed like a single artefact, resting improbably on its bed of mud and sand.

Barry Unsworth, *Stone Virgin* (1985)

❋ ❋ ❋

If you are in Venice long enough to get tired of narrow canals, gondolas, old churches and exquisite palazzi, you could try a trip to the famous Lido. Gustav von Aschenbach in Thomas Mann's Death in Venice *points out that the Lido unites* 'the charms of a luxurious bathing-resort by a southern sea with the immediate nearness of a unique and marvellous city' – *a fact that hasn't changed. In* Dead Lagoon, *however, Michael Dibdin gives a different view of the place.*

Of all the topographical freaks in the lagoon, the Lido had always seemed to Zen the most disturbing. In summer, its vocation as a seaside resort lent the place an illusory air or normality, but in the bleak depths of February its true nature was mercilessly exposed. Here was a perfectly normal contemporary urban scene, with asphalt streets called *Via* this and *Piazza* that, complete with road signs and traffic lights. There was the usual jumble of apartments and villas, offices and hotels, the usual roar of cars and lorries, scooters, bikes and buses. Everything about the place was perfectly banal, in short, except that it was built on an isolated sandbar a few hundred metres wide between the shallow reaches of the lagoon and the open expanses of the Adriatic.

Michael Dibdin, *Dead Lagoon* (1994)

✻ ✻ ✻

One of the features that make the city so unique is the
presence of so many beautiful palazzi. *In* Carnevale,
Michelle Lovric's novel set in the Venice of Byron and
Casanova, we find a useful description of the layout
of the traditional Venetian palazzo.

La Serenissima, as we Venetians call our city, is as beautiful
and practical as a peacock's tail: her beauty is serviceable. It's
a beauty that seduces people to admire, respect – and to pay.
Our beautiful Venetian *palazzi* are pragmatic. My family's little
palazzo, which now stood in front of us, was a microcosm of
those vast airy dwellings wading on the edges of the Grand
Canal. Like them, beneath the decadent, useless loveliness of
its façade was a kind of private manufactory, a living creature,
efficient as a battleship, economical as a convent.

So our *palazzo* consisted of four floors, starting with a *maga-*
zzino, or warehouse, at water level where my father's goods
came in and out at the landing stage on the canal. Above this
was a low-ceilinged *mezzanino* floor where his clerks slaved
over the ledgers and the precious articles were stored away
from the damp depredations of *acqua alta*. Above this was the
piano nobile, which housed the frescoed reception rooms and
large, light bedrooms of my family. Finally, beneath the roof,
the servants had their hot, high domain. The *palazzi* on the
Grand Canal often had two *piani nobili*, one for public and
one for private use. My family could afford such a *palazzo*,
but our position, on a distant and relatively low limb of the
noble Cornaro family tree, would have rendered that extra
piano nobile ostentatious, something my father would never
countenance.

M. R. Lovric, *Carnevale* (2001)

✻ ✻ ✻

One of the most famous palazzi, the Casa Grimani, is here described by one of the most famous writers on the architecture of Venice – John Ruskin. His description still allows one to recognise the building immediately.

Of all the buildings in Venice later in date than the final additions to the Ducal Palace, the noblest is, beyond all question, that which, having been condemned by its proprietor, not many years ago, to be pulled down and sold for the value of its materials, was rescued by the Austrian government, and appropriated – the government officers having no further use for it – to the business of the Post-Office; though still known to the gondolier by its ancient name, the Casa Grimani. It is composed of three storeys of the Corinthian order, at once simple, delicate, and sublime; but on so colossal a scale that the three-storeyed palaces on its right and left only reach to the cornice which marks the level of its first floor. Yet it is not at first perceived to be so vast; and it is only when some expedient is employed to hide it from the eye that by the sudden dwarfing of the whole reach of the Grand Canal, which it commands, we become aware that it is to the majesty of the Casa Grimani that the Rialto itself, and the whole group of neighbouring buildings, owe the greater part of their impressiveness. Nor is the finish of its details less notable than the grandeur of their scale. There is not an erring line, nor a mistaken proportion, throughout its noble front; and the exceeding fineness of the chiselling gives an appearance of lightness to the vast blocks of stone out of whose perfect union that front is composed. The decoration is sparing, but delicate, the first storey only simpler than the rest in that it has pilasters instead of shafts, but all with Corinthian capitals, rich in leafage, and fluted delicately, the rest of the walls flat and smooth and their mouldings sharp and shallow so that the bold shafts look like crystals of beryl running through a rock of quartz.

This palace is the principal type at Venice, and one of the best in Europe, of the central architecture of the Renaissance school.

John Ruskin, *The Stones of Venice, Vol. III* (1867)

❋ ❋ ❋

Another famous palazzo, *once owned by Peggy Guggenheim, now houses the Museum of Modern Art, while its garden holds an unusual secret ...*

In the garden of the *palazzo* that today houses the Museum of Modern Art, there is a tiny graveyard for dogs. Their masters buried them. They loved and mourned them. Their names and nicknames are chiselled into the granite headstones along with their dates of birth and death. Some unknown person places roses here and removes them when they begin to wither. The museum is public, the graveyard private. Many pass by without noticing it. I haven't managed to discover where the Venetians bury their pets otherwise, or whether they do so at all. In the old Lazzaretto, where the little church of Santa Maria di Nazareth once stood, there is a shelter for homeless dogs, lost or abandoned, but not a single grave or headstone.

The owner of the Palazzo Guggenheim maintained that 'for the inhabitants of this city, a funeral without tears is not a real funeral.' She came from far away. She is buried in a graveyard at some distance from the *palazzo* where she once lived with her devoted dogs.

Pedrag Matvejević, *The Other Venice* (2004)
translated by Russell Scott Valentino

❋ ❋ ❋

It's probably most Venetian visitors' dream to stay in a palazzo *rather than a 'vulgar hotel'. In Henry James' novel* The Wings of the Dove, *a young American, Milly Theale, describes the ideal ... which is duly provided for her.*

'At Venice, please, if possible, no dreadful, no vulgar hotel; but if it can be at all managed – you know what I mean – some fine old rooms, wholly independent, for a series of months. Plenty of them, too, and the more interesting the better: part of a palace, historic and picturesque, but strictly inodorous, where we shall be to ourselves, with a cook, don't you know? – with servants, frescoes, tapestries, antiquities, the thorough make-believe of a settlement.' [...]

Palazzo Leporelli held its history still in its great lap, even like a painted idol, a solemn puppet hung about with decorations. Hung about with pictures and relics, the rich revered and served: which brings us back to our truth of a moment ago – the fact that, more than ever, this October morning, awkward novice though she might be, Milly moved slowly to and fro as the priestess of the worship.

Henry James, *The Wings of the Dove* (1902)

✻ ✻ ✻

Another fictional visitor – Patricia Highsmith's very talented Mr Ripley – also enjoys the 'kudos' that comes with living in a palazzo.

'Signor Ripley, one of the young well-to-do American visitors in Italy,' said *Oggi*, 'now lives in a palazzo overlooking San Marco in Venice.' That pleased Tom most of all. He cut out that write-up.

Tom had not thought of it as a 'palace' before, but of course it was what the Italians called a palazzo – a two-storey house of formal design more than two hundred years old, with a main entrance on the Grand Canal approachable only by gondola, with broad stone steps descending into the water, and iron doors that had to be opened by an eight-inch-long key, besides the regular doors behind the iron doors which also took an enormous key. Tom used the less formal 'back door' usually, which was on the Viale San Spiridione, except when he wanted to impress his guests by bringing them to his home in a gondola. The back door – itself fourteen feet high like the stone wall that enclosed the house from the street – led into a garden that was somewhat neglected but still green, and which boasted two gnarled olive trees and a birdbath made of an ancient-looking statue of a naked boy holding a wide shallow bowl. It was just the garden for a Venetian palace, slightly run down, in need of some restoration which it was not going to get, but indelibly beautiful because it had sprung into the world so beautiful more than two hundred years ago. The inside of the house was Tom's ideal of what a civilised bachelor's home should look like, in Venice, at least: a checkerboard black-and-white marble floor downstairs extending from the formal foyer into each room, pink and white marble floor upstairs, furniture that did not resemble furniture at all but an embodiment of cinquecento music played on hautboys, recorders, and violas da gamba. He had his servants – Anna and Ugo, a young Italian couple who had worked for an American in Venice before, so that they knew the difference between a Bloody Mary and a crème de menthe frappé – polish the carved fronts of the armoires and chests and chairs until they seemed alive with dim lustrous lights that moved as one moved around them. The only thing faintly modern was the bathroom. In Tom's bedroom stood a gargantuan bed, broader than it was long. Tom decorated his bedroom with a series of panoramic pictures of Naples from 1540 to about 1880, which he found at an antique store. He had given his undivided attention to decorating his house for more than a week. There was a sureness in his taste now that he had not felt in Rome, and that his Rome apartment had not hinted at. He felt surer of himself now in every way.

Patricia Highsmith, *The Talented Mr Ripley* (1956)

✳ ✳ ✳

Henry James again – in The Aspern Papers – *on a less glamorous specimen of palazzo.*

The gondola stopped, the old palace was there; it was a house of the class which in Venice carries even in extreme dilapidation the dignified name. 'How charming! It's grey and pink!' my companion exclaimed; and that is the most comprehensive description of it. It was not particularly old, only two or three centuries; and it had an air not so much of decay as of quiet discouragement, as if it had rather missed its career. But its wide front, with a stone balcony from end to end of the *piano nobile* or most important floor, was architectural enough, with the aid of various pilasters and arches; and the stucco with which in the intervals it had long ago been endued was rosy in the April afternoon. It overlooked a clean melancholy rather lonely canal, which had a narrow *riva* or convenient footway on either side. 'I don't know why – there are no brick gables,' said Mrs Prest, 'But this corner has seemed to me before more Dutch than Italian, more like Amsterdam than like Venice. It's eccentrically neat, for reasons of its own; and though you may pass on foot scarcely anyone ever thinks of doing so. It's as negative – considering *where* it is – as a Protestant Sunday. Perhaps the people are afraid of the Misses Bordereau. I dare say they have the reputation of witches.'

I forget what answer I made to this – I was given up to two other reflections. The first of these was that if the old lady lived in such a big and imposing house she couldn't be in any sort of misery and therefore wouldn't be tempted by a chance to let a couple of rooms. I expressed this fear to Mrs Prest, who gave me a very straight answer. 'If she didn't live in a very big house how could it be a question of her having rooms to spare? If she were not amply lodged you'd lack grounds to approach her. Besides, a big house here, and especially in this *quartier perdu*, proves nothing at all: it's perfectly consistent with a state of penury. Dilapidated old palazzi, if you'll go out of the way for them, are to be had for five shillings a year. And as for the people who live in them – no, until you have explored Venice socially as much as I have, you can form no idea of their domestic desolation. They live on nothing, for they've nothing to live on.' The other idea that had come into my head was connected with a high blank wall which appeared to confine an expanse of ground on one side of the house. Blank I call it, but it was figured over with patches that please a painter, repaired breaches, crumblings of plaster, extrusions of brick that had turned pink with time.

Henry James, The Aspern Papers (1888)

✳ ✳ ✳

Apart from Murano, one of the most popular islands to visit is San Michele – the cemetery island, where one can pay one's respects to the famous who have chosen to spend their eternity in La Serenissima. We finish this section with three depictions of the island.

The island of San Michele was a walled cemetery, and at first sight it looked impregnable, like a fortress that has risen unexpectedly from the sea. Its sheer walls acted as a sort of dyke, and above them appeared the tops of cypresses, like spikes on a railing. For centuries the Venetian Republic had practised a form of segregation of its sick inhabitants, believing that this would keep the city pure and uncontaminated: the dead on San Michele, lunatics on San Servolo, lepers on San Lazzaro dei Armeni, Jews on the Giudecca. In this way, they created an archipelago of the marginalised, which failed however to protect them from miscegenation or leprosy, from madness or death, or from any other malady or blight. [...]

If the city is split up into districts that maintain the distinction between those of high and those of low estate, the cemetery is divided into sectors, each of which has its own particular style: pantheons hung with ivy for the more aristocratic families;

whitewashed tombs for nuns and monks; lofty tombs for the more valiant of their military heroes; shaded tombs for practitioners of lesser religions; and niches for the plebs. The tombs of the bourgeoisie are the most consummately vulgar of them all: on the headstones of marble, or some marble substitute, there are epitaphs with photographs of the deceased, smiling, their white teeth becoming even whiter as the years go by, since all the other colours are washed out by the weather. Some of these portraits look like X-rays of ectoplasm. [...]

The Venetians seem to harbour a peculiar grudge against their dead. They mock and humiliate them by decorating their graves with bunches of artificial flowers, which degrade the place. Morning light filtered through the sombre foliage of the cypresses, and fell about my shoulders.

Juan Manuel de Prada, *The Tempest* (1997)
translated by Paul Antill

❊ ❊ ❊

Brunetti walked down to the San Zaccaria stop and caught the number 5 boat, which would take him to the cemetery island of San Michele, cutting through the Arsenale and along the back side of the island. He seldom visited the cemetery, somehow not having acquired the cult of the dead so common among Italians.

He had come here in the past; in fact, one of his first memories was of being taken here as a child to help tend the grave of his grandmother, killed in Treviso during the Allied bombing of that city during the war. He remembered how colourful the graves were, blanketed with flowers, and how neat, each precise rectangle separated from the others by razor-edged patches of green. And, in the midst of this, how grim the people, almost all women, who came carrying those armloads of flowers. How drab and shabby they were, as if all their love for colour and neatness was exhausted by the need to care for those spirits in the ground, leaving none left over for themselves.

And now, some thirty-five years later, the graves were just as neat, the flowers still explosive with colour, but the people who passed among the graves looked as if they belonged to the world of the living, were no longer those wraiths of the postwar years. His father's grave was easily found, not too far from Stravinsky. The Russian was safe; he would remain there, untouched, for as long as the cemetery remained or people remembered his music. His father's tenancy was far more precarious, for the time was arriving when his grave would be opened and his bones taken to be put in an ossuary in one of the long, crowded walls of the cemetery.

Donna Leon, Death at La Fenice (1992)

✳ ✳ ✳

From time to time Laura consulted the map. Eventually she said they should get off at the next stop.

'What's here?'

'San Michele,' she said. 'A cemetery.' He could see it now: like Böcklin's *Isle of the Dead*, but symmetrical and neat, and not at all foreboding.

After so long on a boat, the land swayed like the sea. Laura put up her lemon parasol. With the sun so bright, it glowed as if illuminated. All the women, surely, wished they had a parasol, and all the men must have wished they were with the woman who had one. They walked through the gates, entered the curving walls of the island. Beyond this they found themselves in the larger grounds of the cemetery. It was crowded with graves, crammed with flowers. Laura said, 'Diaghilev is buried here. And Stravinsky.'

The first sign they saw, though, was for Ezra Pound. Within the white arrow indicating the way to his grave, someone had written, in black felt tip: 'J Brodsky'. Strictly speaking it was graffiti, but it was very civic-minded too. Officially you were directed towards Pound, but someone had taken it upon themselves to update the canon through a bit of guerrilla action. Pound now led, inexorably, to Brodsky. Jeff had never read Brodsky, but knew he was a big deal, that there were growing numbers of people for whom he – Brodsky – was a bigger attraction than Pound. They came to another sign indicating Pound's grave. Once again, the same person had written 'J Brodsky' in felt pen on the arrow.

It was Pound's grave they saw first, a flat tomb with his name in Roman characters: EZRA POVND. Quite a few flowers. Always good to see the grave of a celebrity, even if it's someone you aren't especially interested in – but it was difficult, these days, to imagine anyone except academics getting excited about Pound. Or maybe he'd got that wrong, maybe there were still kids in their bedrooms, all fired up with the promise of modernism, intent on making it new – whatever the 'it' was.

Brodsky was nearby, within spitting distance: a headstone with his name in Russian and English and his dates: 1940–1996. It wasn't a mess exactly, but there was a touch of Jim Morrison and Père-Lachaise about the scene. There were a couple of tealights, empty except for a last smear of candle wax, and some postcards with messages. Laura picked up one of them. It showed the Grand Canal, but the writing on the back was too blurred by rain and faded by sun to read. A yellow Post-it had been almost completely wiped clean by the elements. It was impossible to say what language the vestiges of words were in, let alone what they had said. By the headstone itself was a little blue plastic bowl, half-full of Biros and pencils. Most of the pens were caked with mud; at a push one or two might have been usable – not to write a poem, but good enough to jot down a phone number.

Laura rummaged in her bag and added a shiny new Biro to the pile. Now someone could write something longer. She even added a few pages from her notebook. The future was a blank page, ready for whoever came after Brodsky and wanted to have their say.

'In India these kids are all the time running up to you,' Laura said. 'All they want and know how to say is "School pen?" They just say it as a question: "School pen?" It's the cutest thing. It's lovely, if you have a pen to give. If you haven't, you feel mean as Scrooge.'

They walked on. It was hot under the parasol, but cooler than not being under it. Diaghilev and Stravinsky were next to each other. At Diaghilev's tomb a similar practice of appropriate tribute was in operation. Pens had been left at the poet's grave; here, people had left ballet shoes. There were three in total, three halves of three pairs, two left and one right. Lots of messages too. Stravinsky's tomb was bare. No one had left a violin or piano or anything.

They waited on the quay for the vaporetto. When it came they squeezed to the back of the boat, watched the island of the dead slide away behind them. After a few minutes there was nothing to see except a thin line of land surrounded by sea and parched sky.

Geoff Dyer, *Jeff in Venice, Death in Varanasi* (2009)

"Streets full of water … "

When American humourist Robert Benchley visited Venice, he sent a telegram to his editor at the New Yorker: "Streets full of water. Please advise." It's a joke that sums up the reality of Venice: the canals are the city's main streets and you can't go very far without boarding a boat. Venetian Tiziano Scarpa describes this everyday Venetian activity for the newcomer.

Prepare to board a vaporetto (in Venetian, *batèo*), stand and wait on the landing stages (*imbarcadèri*): the vaporetto pulls up, giving you a jolt that takes you by surprise like a sudden slap on the back. Climb on board and, again, don't sit down, stay upright on the deck, beneath the external roof; feel with your legs the trembling of the engine in the vaporetto's belly, making your calves vibrate, the roll that constantly forces you to shift the weight of your body from one leg to the other, making you tense and relax muscles you didn't know you had. I should point out to you that on public transport, the vaporetti of the Venetian Public Transport Company (ACTV), you will pay five times as much as a Venetian resident, who can buy a special card, the Cartavenezia, at a much more modest rate.

Tiziano Scarpa, *Venice is a Fish* (2000)
translated by Shaun Whiteside

❊ ❊ ❊

The traditional way of getting around Venice – the gondola – is now the province of those tourists who can afford to hire one ... for half an hour! Gone are the days when visitors such as Lady Chatterley could contemplate having their personal gondola for their entire stay in the city.

They left the car in Mestre, in a garage, and took the regular steamer over to Venice. It was a lovely summer afternoon, the shallow lagoon rippled, the full sunshine made Venice, turning its back to them across the water, look dim.

At the station quay they changed to a gondola, giving the man the address. He was a regular gondolier in a white-and-blue blouse, not very good-looking, not at all impressive.

'Yes! The Villa Esmeralda! Yes! I know it! I have been the gondolier for a gentleman there. But a fair distance out!'

He seemed a rather childish, impetuous fellow. He rowed with a certain exaggerated impetuosity, through the dark side-canals with the horrible, slimy green walls, the canals that go through the poorer quarters, where the washing hangs high up on ropes, and there is a slight, or strong, odour of sewage.

But at last he came to one of the open canals with pavement on either side, and looping bridges, that run straight, at right-angles to the Grand Canal. The two women sat under the little awning, the man was perched above, behind them.

'Are the signorine staying long at the Villa Esmeralda?' he asked, rowing easy, and wiping his perspiring face with a white-and-blue handkerchief.

'Some twenty days: we are both married ladies,' said Hilda, in her curious hushed voice, that made Italian sound so foreign.

'Ah! Twenty days!' said the man. There was a pause. After which he asked: 'Do the signore want a gondolier for the twenty days or so that they will stay in the Villa Esmeralda? Or by the day, or by the week?'

Connie and Hilda considered. In Venice, it is always preferable to have one's own gondola, as it is preferable to have one's own car on land.

D. H. Lawrence, *Lady Chatterley's Lover* (1928)

❊ ❊ ❊

In this gondola ride, from L. P. Hartley's Eustace and Hilda, *the beauties of the water itself are the main focus of the writing.*

They were following a serpentine channel marked by rough wooden posts tipped with pitch, visible, if one stood up, as a dark blue streak in the paler water of the lagoon. Already, to Eustace's distress – for he disliked estuaries – the mud flats were peeping through in places. Soon they were crossing a much wider channel, too deep for posts, almost a river; he could hear the current gurgling against the boat, carrying it out of its course. Then the posts wound into view again, and the gondola followed under the long wall of the Arsenal, a huge pink rampart stained white with salty sweat. Other islands appeared on their right – Burano, to whose inhabitants Silvestro made some slighting reference, and far away, high in the haze, Torcello and the pine trees of San Francesco del Deserto. Silvestro stopped rowing to announce them, as though they were celebrities arriving at a party. Straight ahead a long garden wall stretched into the lagoon, trees overhung it; a water-gate gave the impression of depths of green within, restful to the eye besieged with pink and blue.

Suddenly, where no opening in the left-hand bastion seemed possible, an opening appeared; into it they swung, leaving the lagoon behind them. Eustace stood up to take a last look at it, framed in the aperture. By comparison the canal seemed lightless and confined and noisy; washing hung out in festoons; long window boxes sported innumerable aspidistras (the patron plant of Venice, Lady Nelly had called it) in somewhat garish pots; canaries lustily gave tongue, and the people on the pavement greeted or admonished each other raucously across great distances. [...]

Soon his eye was drawn by the sunlight at the end of the canal. Above and below the slender bridge that spanned it, the sunshine was at its glorious and exciting game, playing with the blue and white in the water and the blue and white in the sky, gathering into itself and giving out again all the confused movement of the two elements. The moment before they reached the bridge was tense with the radiance waiting to receive them, and when they shot through it into the sparkling water of the great basin, heaving under them with a deep-sea strength of purpose, Eustace felt the illumination pierce him like a pang.

Relaxed and happy Eustace had only a casual eye for the man-made splendours of the Grand Canal, exhibiting themselves with serene self-confidence, an epic procession, but a pageant without drama.

L.P. Hartley, *Eustace and Hilda* (1958)

✳ ✳ ✳

Many of the gondola rides depicted in literature turn out to be less than the romantic ideal – as in this short extract from The Talented Mr Ripley.

Marge wanted a private gondola, of course, not the regular ferry-service gondola that took people over ten at a time from San Marco's to the steps of Santa Maria della Salute, so they engaged a private gondola. It was one-thirty in the morning. Tom had a dark brown taste in his mouth from too many espressos, his heart was fluttering like bird wings, and he did not expect to be able to sleep until dawn. He felt exhausted, and lay back in the gondola's seat about as languidly as Marge, careful to keep his thigh from touching hers. Marge was still in ebullient spirits, entertaining herself now with a monologue about the sunrise in Venice, which she had apparently seen on some other visit. The gentle rocking of the boat and the rhythmic thrusts of the gondolier's oar made Tom feel slightly sickish. The expanse of water between the San Marco boat stop and his steps seemed interminable.

The steps were covered now except for the upper two, and the water swept just over the surface of the third step, stirring its moss in a disgusting way. [...]

It was not at all a beautiful night. It was chilly, and a slimy little rain had started falling.

Patricia Highsmith, *The Talented Mr Ripley* (1956)

❖ ❖ ❖

Thomas Mann's Death in Venice *describes the rather seedy gondola ride of the aging Gustav von Aschenbach in pursuit of Tadzio, the young boy with whose beauty he has become obsessed.*

Tadzio and his sisters at length took a gondola. Ashenbach hid behind a portico or fountain while they embarked and directly they pushed off did the same. In a furtive whisper he told the boatman he would tip him well to follow at a little distance the other gondola, just rounding a corner, and fairly sickened at the man's quick, sly grasp and ready acceptance of the go-between's role.

Leaning back among soft, black cushions he swayed gently in the wake of the other black-snouted bark, to which the strength of his passion chained him. Sometimes it passed from his view, and then he was assailed by an anguish of unrest. But his guide appeared to have long practice in affairs like these; always, by dint of short cuts or deft manoeuvres, he contrived to overtake the coveted sight. The air was heavy and foul, the sun burnt down through a slate-coloured haze. Water slapped gurgling against wood and stone. The gondolier's cry, half warning, half salute, was answered with singular accord from far within the silence of the labyrinth. They passed little gardens high up the crumbling wall, hung with clustering white and purple flowers that sent down an odour of almonds. Moorish lattices showed shadowy in the gloom. The marble steps of a church descended into the canal, and on them a beggar squatted, displaying his misery to view, showing the whites of his eyes, holding out his hat for alms. Farther on a dealer in antiquities cringed before his lair, inviting the passer-by to enter and be duped. Yes, this was Venice, this the fair frailty that fawned and that betrayed, half fairy-tale, half snare; the city in whose stagnating air the art of painting once put forth so lusty a growth, and where musicians were moved to accords so weirdly lulling and lascivious. Our adventurer felt his senses wooed by this voluptuousness of sight and sound, tasted his secret knowledge that the city sickened and hid its sickness for love of gain, and bent an ever more unbridled leer on the gondola that glided on before him.

Thomas Mann, *Death in Venice* (1912)
translated by H. T. Lowe-Porter

✳ ✳ ✳

And even Marcel Proust chooses the less romantic, poorer districts for this gondola ride described in one of the later volumes of In Search of Lost Time.

My gondola followed the course of the small canals; like the mysterious hand of a genie leading me through the maze of this oriental city, they seemed, as I advanced, to be cutting a path for me through the heart of a crowded quarter which they bisected, barely parting, with a slender furrow arbitrarily traced, the tall houses with their tiny Moorish windows; and as though the magic guide had been holding a candle in his hand and were lighting the way for me, they kept casting ahead of them a ray of sunlight for which they cleared a route. One felt that between the mean dwellings which the canal had just parted, and which otherwise would have formed a compact whole, no open space had been reserved; so that a campanile or a garden trellis vertically overhung the *rio*, as in a flooded city. But, for both churches and gardens, thanks to the same trans-position as in the Grand Canal, the sea so readily served as a means of communication, as substitute for street or alley, that on either side of the *canaletto* the belfries rose from the water in this poor and populous district like those of humble and much-frequented parish churches bearing the stamp of their necessity, of their use by crowds of simple folk, the gardens traversed by the canal cutting trailed their startled leaves and fruit in the water, and on the ledges of the houses whose crudely cut stone was still rough as though it had only just been sawn, urchins surprised by the gondola sat back trying to keep their balance and allowing their legs to dangle vertically, like sailors seated upon a swing-bridge the two halves of which have been swung apart, allowing the sea to pass between them. Now and again would appear a handsomer building that happened to be there like a surprise in a box which one has just opened, a little ivory temple with its Corinthian columns and an alle-gorical statue on its pediment, somewhat out of place among the ordinary surroundings in the midst of which, for all that we tried to make space for it, the peristyle with which the canal had provided it retained the look of a landing-stage for market gardeners. I had the impression, which my desire strengthened further, of not being outside, but of entering more and more into the depths of something secret, because each time I found something new which came to place itself on one side of me or the other, a small monument or an unexpected *campo*, keeping the surprised expression of beautiful things which one sees for the first time and of which one doesn't yet perfectly understand the intended purpose or the utility.

Marcel Proust, *The Fugitive* (1925)
translated by C.K. Scott Moncrieff and Terence Kilmartin
(revised by D.J. Enright)

❧ ❧ ❧

And another glimpse of a gondola ride 'off the beaten track' ...

They had turned off the Grand Canal into another of the myriad small waterways that led from it. There was quiet here, the *vaporetti* could not get down it and Nicolò had to handle the gondola carefully, sending his whistle ahead, or using his oar to push past a motor-boat. 'They do such damage, scraping the walls. There is war, Pippa, between the gondolas and the water-taxis.' They passed a barge tied up with a wonderful display of vegetables; people with baskets were buying. Another barge passed them, heaped with barrels and a goat loose on it. They rounded a corner into deeper quiet.

Both banks were lined with houses, not huddled together, most with slit windows as if they turned their backs on the canal, and had high walls showing a glimpse of gardens behind them: trees, fig and acacia, creepers, roses and wisteria hanging over the walls. All had steps going down to the water, some with gondola posts where private smart motor-boats were moored and heavy doors kept firmly shut. Very special people must live here, thought Pippa.

Rumer Godden, Pippa Passes (1995)

❉ ❉ ❉

In Libby Purves's novel More Lives Than One, *a party of school-children are taken on an unforgettable night-time gondola adventure.*

Outside again, the cold air refreshed them. Kit led them by his silken cord down through the alleys to the little canal of San Zulian, where he told them to wait while he swung down onto a pontoon. Half a dozen gondolas gleamed darker black against the night and as they bobbed on the water, their high prows like silver combs caught the light from a single street lamp. It was quieter here, and the fifteen masked children stood shivering slightly, their silhouettes odd and humped where the black cloaks rested on the padded shoulders of their anoraks. After a brief rapid conversation, Kit called them down. [...]

More of them were shuddering now from the cold and the insecurity of being down on the canal, smelling it, wobbling on its ripples. It seemed a more vital, threatening element now than when they looked at it from firm ground or from the high deck of a *vaporetto*.

'Weird,' said Joe Baldwin quietly, speaking for them all.

Kit spoke again briefly to the four gondoliers, who nodded and grinned. Then they pushed off, one by one, leaning to their single oars with lounging casual grace.

All through their various lives, each of the fifteen children would remember that night and that ride. Some talked of it to their own children: of the way the long boats slid silently under arched bridges and through dark ravines of tall houses, of the snatches of music that echoed plaintively round distant corners, of the splashing of the oar and the ghostly cry of 'Ey-o!' loosed by their gondolier at each sharp turn.

They would remember the excitement and the fear as one dim, dank passage followed another, and the relief of the moment when suddenly they came out onto the Grand Canal and all was light and glory after the murderous darkness of the back canals. Even those who did not talk of it remembered; they wrote their diaries that night, kept them through the careless teenage years, found them again in the detritus of some house move, read them again and put them carefully aside. As Kit had intended, the night and the city stayed with the children for good. In that half-hour each laid down a layer of necessary splendour, a cushion to stay hidden but perennially comforting beneath the hard banality of life.

Libby Purves, *More Lives Than One* (1998)

✻ ✻ ✻

The prevalence of water and humidity in Venice provides endless problems for the fabric of the buildings. But Pedrag Matvejević finds beauty in the watery decay.

When undisturbed, the water of the canals yields to sunshine and palace shade, to a ceaseless play of light and shadow. The slender vegetal layer along the walls and steps marks the boundary of the moisture's reach. It was lower in the past than it is today. At the top the algae look like moss, at the bottom like wild grass. It is the same deep green I saw on the cloak of the saint in an old church at Campo San Barnaba and in a small chapel at Cannaregio. The moisture seeps into everything – into walls and stones, wood, iron and bricks. Into the spirit. Beside a jetty is a plank bridge, worm-eaten and turgid: the water inside keeps the water outside from entering. Everything rots – the old planks, the trunks beneath the *fondamenta*, the bollards on the jetty, the bailers in the boats, the dried-out oars. Even the stones rot, though in a different way, more slowly, unnoticeably. Inside the rock, wood and brick, the water itself grows old. Can its age be determined?

Rust bites into the iron, here at great depth, there on the surface. Its colour varies from brown to red to black. In places it is 'russet rust' (we find these colours, these nuances, in the late canvases of Titian). Layers of rust and patina distort the metal objects – gates, plaques, grilles and fences, locks and keys. One cannot say precisely why patina covers some while others are eaten by rust, inside and out.

In the places most exposed to the water, humidity, evaporation, haze and decay, one discovers links between rust and patina that are perhaps more subtle and secretive, like games broken off and re-begun, attraction and repulsion complementing each other, the remains of some unknown alphabet one tries in vain to decipher. One sees glimpses of ill-defined and unanticipated outlines, irregular and irreducible shapes, improbable, inexplicable figures. They approach each other and, somehow, elude each other. When the rust darkens and begins to decay and the patina pales and begins to fall away, they again become similar, equally dependent and superfluous. It is a fate shared by nearly all the metals, each according to its measure and disposition – iron, copper, lead. Thus as well do the alloys of brass and bronze resist age and disrepair. Gold, too, changes with time, as if its own shadow were suspended above it or had crept inside. Silver loses some of its sheen, all its reflection, its covering exchanged for a dingy coat, its body, so to speak, grown thin.

The rust of Venice is sumptuous; the patina like gilding.

Pedrag Matvejević, *The Other Venice* (2004)
translated by Russell Scott Valentino

❋ ❋ ❋

The logistics of running a city whose roads are made of water are quite different from those of a 'normal' city. There's the problem of rubbish collection and disposal ... and then the maintenance and repair of the 'roads' ...

One of the things that had charmed Henchard from his first days in the city was the smoothly working perfection of Venetian civic arrangements. All the problems of life in a watery metropolis had been solved long ago. Since there were no fields, no orchards, no cows or pigs or chickens in this city of stone, everything had to come from the mainland. And of course since there was no extra land anywhere for the disposal of rubbish, every scrap of refuse had to be removed by boat. Henchard had seen rubbish carts hoisted over the seagoing boats of the Netturbini on the edge of the Riva degli Schiavoni, he had seen the bottoms fall open and the debris tumble out. He had seen the fully laden boats chug away into the lagoon.

Out there somewhere, far from the city, they dropped their cargoes. And then, freed of their trash from yesterday – all their smelly garbage and used diapers and tin cans and empty bottles and occasional severed heads and arms and legs – the citizens of Venice could begin the day as fresh and spotless as newborn babes.

Jane Langton, *The Thief of Venice* (1999)

✳ ✳ ✳

A little past San Ivo a canal was being dredged, a dirty job saved for winter, when no visitors were here to see. Wooden planks dammed each end so big rubber hoses could pump out the water, leaving a floor of mud, just a few feet down, where workmen in boots were shovelling muck and debris into carts. The mud covered everything, spattering the workers' blue coveralls, hanging in clots on the canal walls, just below the line of moss. [...]

I watched the workmen sliding in the wet muck. In a few days they'd be finished, the garbage and the smell gone, and the water would flood back, the surface a mirror again, dazzling, so that when you came to it, around the corner, you felt you were stepping into a painting.

Joseph Kanon, *Alibi* (2005)

❊ ❊ ❊

But forgetting about the problems of a watery city,
we'll take a couple of pleasant – and informative –
trips out to the islands with Barry Unsworth and
Michael Dibdin.

It was a day of bright sunshine, clear enough, though the sun
was softened by the remnants of the night's mists. Once past
San Michele and Murano they were in the open, the great
expanse of the Lagoon before and all around them, a vast glimmering sheet, patterned by its shallows, streaked here and there
with rippling flashes where mud flats broke the surface; elsewhere unblemished, pale blue, with a soft shine to it as though
wiped with oil.

The boat steamed north-east towards Mazzorbo following
the staked-out line of the deep-water channel. Raikes strained
his eyes eastward across the shifting glimmers of the surface to
where the brightness gathered and dazzled. He could make out
the long shape of the Lido and the campanile of San Nicolò.
Small islands, mere mudbanks tufted with vegetation, were
discernible on both sides; others, more distant, were half lost in
the haze, darker impurities in the clouded liquid of the horizon.
To the east a mile or two away he thought he identified the
island gardens of La Vignola and Sant'Erasmo which supply
Venice with vegetables. [...]

The boat passed close to an island he remembered, the
sad, abandoned San Giacomo in the Marsh, with its broken
walls, grassed-over mounds of rubble and listing birch trees.
'Appropriate name,' he said to Wiseman. 'It looks like a marsh,
doesn't it? A marsh that someone was once foolish enough to
build on.'

They were standing towards the stern, where it was roofed
but open at the sides. Wiseman had turned up the collar of his
light tweed overcoat. With his hair ruffled by the sea breeze

and his cheeks rosy from the fresh air, he looked more than ever like an older-generation cherub, a worn cupid caught in some sportive billows aimed by Venus. 'It had a population of several thousand at one time,' he said. 'Hard to believe now, isn't it? The church was built by Carducci. They didn't keep up the sea walls. Shortage of cash, or so they say – it's the province of the Magistura alla Aqua. There are drowning islands all over the Lagoon, and quite a few underneath the water, of course, like Costanziaca for example, which was a flourishing place long before San Marco was thought of, with churches and monasteries – it was a place of pilgrimage famous throughout Italy. Then the tides just slowly made a marsh of it. The waters closed over it some time in the eighteenth century, I think.'

They were approaching Mazzorbo now, with the campanile of Santa Caterina rising immediately before them. The *moto-scafo* turned at right angles up the wide canal, stopped at the Burano landing stage where it deposited Raikes and Wiseman. They stood for some moments on the jetty, watching the boat nose out again towards Torcello.

Barry Unsworth, *Stone Virgin* (1985)

✻ ✻ ✻

The launch roared off again through the back canals of Dorso-duro, narrowly avoiding a collision with a taxi full of fat men with video cameras and skinny women in furs, past tiny intricate palaces and vast abandoned churches, under bridges so low they had to duck and through gaps so narrow they touched the fenders of the moored boats. Then at last, with a dramatic suddenness that took Zen's breath away, they emerged into the Giudecca channel, the deepest and broadest of all the waterways within the city.

The wind seemed much stronger here, chopping up the water into short, hard waves which shattered under the hull of the launch. The car ferry to Alexandria was steaming slowly down the channel, and Martufò sent the launch veering dangerously close under the towering bows of the huge vessel, keeling over with the force of the turn, the gunwales sunk in the surging torrent of white water. Then they were across the channel and into the sheltered canals separating the Giudecca from the *sacce*.

These small islands were some of the last areas in the city to be built on, remaining undeveloped until the 1960s. Zen could remember rowing across to them when they were still a green oasis of allotments and meadows. Now Sacca Fisola was covered in streets and squares, shops, schools, playgrounds and six-storey apartment blocks. Except for the eerie absence of traffic, it was all exactly identical to suburbs of the same period in any mainland city. But here there were no cars, no lorries, no motorbikes or scooters. The children played in the street, just as children everywhere had done a century earlier, but in a street flanked by the sort of brutalist architecture associated with chaotic parking, constant horns, revving two-strokes and blaring car radios. Here, the only sound was the lapping of the water at the shore. The overall effect was extremely unsettling, as though the whole thing were a hoax of some kind.

Michael Dibdin, *Dead Lagoon* (1994)

✳ ✳ ✳

A gondola trip, especially at night, can have a dream-like quality – there is an 'unreal' quality to the city. Here's a final trip along the waterways with Charles Dickens ... a trip in which reality and dream mingle

Before I knew by what, or how, I found we were gliding up a street – a phantom street, the houses rising on both sides, from the water, and the black boat gliding on beneath their windows. Lights were shining from some of these casements, plumbing the depth of the black stream with their reflected rays, but all was profoundly silent.

So we advanced into this ghostly city, continuing to hold our course through narrow streets and lanes, all filled and flowing with water. Some of the corners where our way branched off were so acute and narrow that it seemed impossible for the long slender boat to turn them; but the rowers, with a melodious cry of warning, sent it skimming on without a pause. Sometimes the rowers of another black boat like our own echoed the cry, and slackening their speed (as I thought we did ours) would come flitting past us like a dark shadow. Other boats, of the same sombre hue, were lying moored, I thought, to painted pillars, near to dark mysterious doors that opened straight upon the water. Some of these were empty; in some, the rowers lay asleep; towards one, I saw some figures coming down a gloomy archway from the interior of a palace, gaily dressed and attended by torch-bearers. It was but a glimpse I had of them, for a bridge, so low and close upon the boat that it seemed ready to fall down and crush us – one of the many bridges that perplexed the Dream – blotted them out instantly. On we went, floating towards the heart of this strange place – with water all about us where never water was elsewhere – clusters of houses, churches, heaps of stately buildings growing out of it – and, everywhere, the same extraordinary silence.

Presently, we shot across a broad and open stream and passing, as I thought, before a spacious paved quay, where the bright lamps with which it was illuminated showed long rows of arches and pillars, of ponderous construction and great strength, but as light to the eye as garlands of hoarfrost or gossamer – and where, for the first time, I saw people walking – arrived at a flight of steps leading from the water to a large mansion where, having passed through corridors and galleries innumerable, I lay down to rest, listening to the black boats stealing up and down below the window on the rippling water, till I fell asleep.

Charles Dickens, 'An Italian Dream', in *Pictures from Italy* (1846)

Sights, sounds, smells ...
and that Venetian weather

Pippa was woken by the sound of Nicolò's oar in the water. He was standing on the stern, the gondola was moving. [...]

It was the earliest of early mornings. The sun had just risen and Venice was a city of light and air, of glittering water, of domes that seemed to rise lightly, finding the sunlight as bubbles find prisms of light in their transparent shells. That was what her grandfather's old book had described and, It's true, thought Pippa again, not only illumined but drenched in light. The dark shadows of the night had gone, there was no darkness now under the bridges. The early morning shone, shimmering like her moonstone but with the colours of a rose opal set clear against the sun.

The deepest shadows had a tone of gold, the highest a light of silver. Pippa looked and looked, herself forgotten, then Nicolò sang a soft '*Ohé*' as he avoided the vegetable barge.

Rumer Godden, *Pippa Passes* (1994)

✳ ✳ ✳

An exquisite early morning in Venice ... and the practical reality of the vegetable barge. The next extract, from Joseph Kanon's Alibi, *focuses mainly on the more practical sights and sounds of the morning-time city, but with a touch of poetry.*

Venice is often said to be a dream, but at that hour, when there is no one out, no sounds but your own steps, it is really so, no longer metaphor – whatever separates the actual paving stones from the alleys in your mind dissolves. The morning mist and the gothic shapes from childhood stories have something to do with this, the rocking slap of boats on the water, tugging at their mooring poles, but mostly it's the emptiness. The campos and largos are deserted, the buoy marker lights in the lagoon undisturbed by wakes, the noisy day, when the visitors fan out into the calles from the Piazzale Roma, still just a single echo. Things appear in that hour the way they do in sleep, gliding unconnected from one to the next, bolted garden door to shadowy church steps to shuttered shop-window, no more substantial than fragments of mist.

The walk was always the same. First down along the Zattere, past the lonely vaporetto stations. Just before the Stazione Marittima I would turn into the calle leading to San Sebastiano, Veronese's church, and a bar for stazione workers that was always open by the time I got there, the windows already moist with steam hissing from the coffee machines. The other customers, in blue workers' coveralls bulked with sweaters underneath, would nod from their spots at the bar, taking in the army coat, then ignore me, turning back to their coffee and cigarettes, voices kept low, as if someone were still sleeping upstairs. Even at that hour a few were tossing back brandies. The coffee had been cut with something – chicory? acorns? – but was still strong enough to jolt me awake, and standing there with a first cigarette, suddenly alert to everything – the steamed windows, the whiff of scalded milk, isolated words of dialect – it seemed to me that I'd never been asleep at all.

Outside there were a few more people – a boy in a waiter's uniform heading toward one of the hotels, an old woman in a fur coat coaxing a dog to pee, a priest with his hands in his sleeves, staying warm, all the insomniacs and early risers I'd never seen before I became one of them. I supposed that if I headed over to the Rialto I could see the fish stalls being set up and the boats unloading, the early-morning working world, but I preferred the empty dream city. From San Sebastiano it was a straight path, only slightly angled by bridges, to Campo San Barnaba. No produce market yet, just a man hurrying toward the traghetto station, perhaps still not home from the night before. Then right toward the Accademia, following the natural course of the streets the way water runs in canals, looping finally around the museum, then through the back alleys toward Salute, not a soul in sight again, past the great swirling church and out along the fundaments to the tip. Here, huddled in my coat with my back against the old customs house, I sat for hours looking across the water to the postcard everyone knew – Ruskin's waves of marble, the gilt of San Marco catching the first morning sun, the columned landing stage filled with boat traffic, all the beautiful buildings rising out of the water, out of consciousness, the city's last dream.

Joseph Kanon, *Alibi* (2005)

✳ ✳ ✳

Taking us back in time, Michelle Lovric recreates the sights, sounds and smells that Byron would have experienced on a morning walk through Venice.

On that first morning, Byron must have continued to hear the Venice I could not describe for him for it is necessary to experience it for one's self. As he passed through the markets he would have heard the thud of hatchets decapitating a thousand artichokes in a single morning, the struggles of boiling water in kettles. He would have heard the wooden spatulas raking through hot nuts roasting in tin drums. From open doors in the laundrywomen's houses would have issued the hiss of irons nosing through the ruffles of the ladies' linen. He must have heard the early violins musing through the windows of the *Conservatorio*. He would have stopped for a moment, there, looking up at the graceful windows.

In the morning-blooming cafés the waiters would have unfurled their tablecloths with a flourish as he passed, and the fragrance of soap dried in sunshine would have flown up to meet his twitching nose. The waiters would have bowed to him, prouder than dukes in their clean frock coats. I know that he passed through the Merceria, tapestried with cloth-of-gold, rich damasks and silks which the shops draped from their first floors. He must have breathed in the perfumes and savoury scents from the apothecary shops. He must have dandled a finger in at least one of the shopkeepers' noisy cages of nightingales. He probably stood at a marble counter and drank a glass of orange juice red as blood. As he crossed bridges he would have trailed his fingers along elaborate railings warmed by the sun.

Byron walked into seduction.

M. R. Lovric, *Carnevale* (2001)

✳ ✳ ✳

In case one gets carried away with the poetic and sensuous side of the city, here's Thomas Mann describing an unpleasantly sultry Venetian afternoon.

In the afternoon he spent two hours in his room, then took the *vaporetto* to Venice, across the foul-smelling lagoon. He got out at San Marco, had his tea in the Piazza, and then, as his custom was, took a walk through the streets. But this walk of his brought about nothing less than a revolution in his mood and an entire change in all his plans.

There was a hateful sultriness in the narrow streets. The air was so heavy that all the manifold smells wafted out of houses, shops, and cook-shops – smells of oil, perfumery, and so forth – hung low, like exhalations, not dissipating. Cigarette smoke seemed to stand in the air, it drifted so slowly away. To-day the crowd in these narrow lanes oppressed the stroller instead of diverting him. The longer he walked, the more was he in tortures under that state, which is the product of the sea air and the sirocco and which excites and enervates at once. He perspired painfully. His eyes rebelled, his chest was heavy, he felt feverish, the blood throbbed in his temples. He fled from the huddled, narrow streets of the commercial city, crossed many bridges, and came into the poor quarter of Venice. Beggars waylaid him, the canals sickened him with their evil exhalations. He reached a quiet square, one of those that exist at the city's heart, forsaken of God and man; there he rested awhile on the margin of a fountain, wiped his brow, and admitted to himself that he must be gone.

For the second time, and now quite definitely, the city proved that in certain weathers it could be directly inimical to his health. Nothing but sheer unreasoning obstinacy would linger on, hoping for an unprophesiable change in the wind.

Thomas Mann, *Death in Venice* (1912)
translated by H. T. Lowe-Porter

✻ ✻ ✻

But the evenings can be magical, whatever the weather, as in these three gems – by Barry Unsworth, Daphne du Maurier, and Caryl Phillips.

Raikes decided to walk a little before getting the *vaporetto*. It was just after ten – a time of evening he had always liked in Venice.

Away from the main thoroughfares the streets were quiet, the lamplight took on a selective, deceiving quality, hiding much that was decayed, touching with sudden caress a stretch of canal, the perfect ellipse of bridge and reflection, and broken glitters where a boat had passed. Aided by this light one could ignore the damp and desolation emanating from ground-floor windows and ruinous boat gates, abandoned as life retreated higher, see only the beauties of the Renaissance brickwork, the exquisite proportions of the house fronts. Time the despoiler had not much hurt the city's beauty, but this was best seen now in ambiguous lights.

He walked in the general direction of San Marco, keeping north of the square. After some time, he found himself at the bridge behind the Basilica. A cruise boat, her decks hung with lights, passed slowly across his line of vision, emerging from the Giudecca Canal towards the open sea beyond. For a moment or two he saw her brilliant upper deck, towering behind the Bridge of Sighs, then she had slid noiselessly out of sight, cut off by the arcades of the Ducal Palace. Floodlighting lay in zones on the canal, flickering at the edges where the water lapped, like a message too rapid to be decoded.

Barry Unsworth, *Stone Virgin* (1985)

✳ ✳ ✳

The soft humidity of the evening, so pleasant to walk about in earlier, had turned to rain. The strolling tourists had melted away. One or two people hurried by under umbrellas. This is what the inhabitants who live here see, he thought. This is the true life. Empty streets by night, the dank stillness of a stagnant canal beneath shuttered houses. The rest is a bright façade put on for show, glittering by sunlight.

Laura joined him and they walked away together in silence, and emerging presently behind the ducal palace came out into the Piazza San Marco. The rain was heavy now, and they sought shelter with the few remaining stragglers under the colonnades.

The orchestras had packed up for the evening. The tables were bare. Chairs had been turned upside down.

The experts are right, he thought. Venice is sinking. The whole city is slowly dying. One day the tourists will travel here by boat to peer down into the waters, and they will see pillars and columns and marble far, far beneath them, slime and mud covering for brief moments a lost underworld of stone. Their heels made a ringing sound on the pavement and the rain splashed from the gutterings above. A fine ending to an evening that had started with brave hope, with innocence.

Daphne du Maurier, *Don't Look Now* (1971)

* * *

I dressed quickly and soon found myself on the wintry Rialto bridge, from whose vantage point I was able to watch a lean cat scurry noiselessly into a blind alley. I had grown extremely fond of the city under the moon, for it was at such moments that I truly appreciated the full grandeur of her silent majesty. Only the occasional tolling of bells trespassed upon the night, but their song, together with the sister sound of water swirling and sighing, created the most wondrous accompaniment to the silence. And then, of course, there was the moonlight, which produced spellbinding patterns as it struck the water, illuminating buildings here, and withholding its light there. Some corners of Venice appeared to have been specially chosen to be blessed with this essential gift of light and shadow.

Caryl Phillips, *The Nature of Blood* (1997)

* * *

Two short pieces on the sounds of Venice – from John Berendt and Tiziano Scarpa.

Footsteps and voices were, in fact, the dominant sounds in Venice, since there were no cars to drown them out and very little vegetation to absorb them. Voices carried with startling clarity through the stone-paved squares and alleys. A few fleeting words spoken in the house across the *calle* sounded surprisingly close, as if they had been uttered by someone in the same room. In the early evenings, people gathered in clusters to gossip in Strada Nuova, the main street of Cannaregio, and the sound of their mingled conversations rose in the air like the buzz of a cocktail party in a large room.

John Berendt, *City of Falling Angels* (2005)

✳ ✳ ✳

Foghorns enlarge the far-off ships, expanding the port through the air.

The depredations of the cats wake you up at night. They challenge one another to duels, hissing in each other's faces, yowling oestrous miaows. [...]

The take-off of the pigeons whirls like the ignition of a broken-winded engine, a gear failing to engage. The sparrows silently steal your crisps as you enjoy an outdoor aperitif.

In the summer the electric microsaws of the cicadas act as spies, informing headquarters about the gardens hidden among the houses. The secret services have scattered them about the place like electronic bugs dropped from helicopters.

The gulls wheel screeching above the market stalls of Santa Margherita, the fishmongers throw flying fish through the air, feather-light sardines, silver fish against the blue sky: the gulls swallow them mid-flight. [...]

Go down the Rialto Bridge on the side of the market. Close your eyes as you walk: listen to the Babel of languages spoken by tourists from all over the world, concentrated along fifty metres of *calle*. [...]

Your day is sliced into hours and half-hours by the peal of the bells. At midnight the mother of all bells booms out: the *marangona* of St Mark's campanile commands silence.

Tiziano Scarpa, *Venice is a Fish* (2000)
translated by Shaun Whiteside

✽ ✽ ✽

And now a look at some typical Venetian weather to expect at various times of year, starting with two 'miniatures' on Summer.

The weather changed, the stubborn storm yielded, and the summer sunshine, baffled for many days, but now hot and almost vindictive, came into its own again and, with an almost audible paean, a suffusion of bright sound that was one with the bright colour, took large possession. Venice glowed and plashed and called and chimed again; the air was like a clap of hands, and the scattered pinks, yellows, blues, sea-greens, were like a hanging-out of vivid stuffs, a laying down of fine carpets.

Henry James, *The Wings of the Dove* (1902)

✽ ✽ ✽

Now daily the naked god with cheeks aflame drove his four fire-breathing steeds through heaven's spaces; and with him streamed the strong east wind that fluttered his yellow locks. A sheen, like winter satin, lay over all the idly rolling sea's expanse. The sand was burning hot. Awnings of rust-coloured canvas were spanned before the bathing-huts, under the ether's quivering silver-blue; one spent the morning hours within the small, sharp square of shadow they purveyed. But evening too was rarely lovely: balsamic with the breath of flowers and shrubs from the near-by park, while overhead the constellations circled in their spheres, and the murmuring of the night-girded sea swelled softly up and whispered to the soul. Such nights as these contained the joyful promise of a sunlit morrow, brim-full of sweetly ordered idleness, studded thick with countless precious possibilities.

Thomas Mann, *Death in Venice* (1912)
translated by H. T. Lowe-Porter

✽ ✽ ✽

*Summer turns into autumn ... Something on the
September weather by L. P. Hartley.*

The days that followed were languid with sirocco. The weather
broke, as it often did in September; masses of cloud piled themselves up and hung, huge fists and fingers of vapour, motionless
over the city, bringing out all that was grey and sullen in the roofs
and walls of Venice. Looking down from his window, Eustace
could see puddles and the shiny black of umbrellas, oil-skins,
sou'westers, and galoshes. The wind blew in sudden gusts, and
the creepers, the Virginia and wisteria which swarmed up the
sides of the houses, writhed and shivered convulsively. Even in
the Grand Canal untamed billows slapped against the gondola
and sometimes splashed into it; visits on foot to the Piazza were
diversified with sudden dashes to take cover.

Eustace had the almost unique experienced of seeing Lady
Nelly hurry and even get sprinkled with a few drops of rain.
Then without warning the sun would come out, and Venice
would once again put on its summer look, enhanced by a million
sparkles from every dripping surface. And all the time the heat
reigned unabated; indeed, increased towards evening when the
sirocco, just when it was needed most, would die away, leaving
behind all the lassitude of its presence without the stimulus of
its movement. Indoors, the walls sweated and ran with salty
damp, and the mosquitoes redoubled their attack.

L.P. Hartley, *Eustace and Hilda* (1958)

✳ ✳ ✳

Autumn is the season of the dreaded acqua alta – *the
'high water' that periodically floods the vulnerable
city when high rubber boots are absolutely* de rigeur.

In October the rains came and those who knew the significance
of such matters cast calculating eyes at the mark on the base
of the campanile in the Piazza which measures the height the
waters reached on November 4th 1966.

Acqua alta, the curse of Venice, for the waters which rise ever higher from the levels of the lagoon become lethal when driven by a following wind. In the Piazza San Marco the raised trestles, by which visitors and natives make their tottering or practised way round the square, were already in place.

Julia had accepted an invitation to dine with the Monsignore. She had set out and returned to put on green rubber boots, the hallmark of those native to the city.

Sally Vickers, *Miss Garnet's Angel* (2000)

✻ ✻ ✻

And some more rain ...

The rain was heavy and relentless in the garden of the palace; it fell on the decapitated marble statues, and into the basin of the fountain, splashing so furiously that it drowned out the refrain of the jet. It was raining on the canals, water lashing water, a violent baptism, of which there had been no prior notice, but which, nevertheless, the canals received with unanimity and the same goodwill with which they received the water from wash-basins and urinals; it was raining on canals which very soon would again run out of control; it was raining on all the little streets of Venice, and on the suddenly deserted squares under the arcades of which horrified tourists, with their hats and bells, stood aghast at the sheer weight of water that would ruin their carnival celebrations.

Juan Manuel de Prada, *The Tempest*
translated by Paul Antill

✻ ✻ ✻

Two Venetian residents give us the factual picture of living with the acqua alta. *First, English novelist Michelle Lovric then Venetian poet, novelist and playwright Tiziano Scarpa.*

Late October. Other parts of Italy start thinking of mushrooms, chestnuts, getting the wood chopped and stacked. There is, I assume, a satisfying feeling of building the stockade against the traditional enemies of cold and hunger.

But in Venice, we have only one true enemy: water. As the year wanes, damp is our condition, our mood, our destiny. It's not just the streets that are weighted with water: so is the misty air, so are the bricks, which bloom a white efflorescence of salt. It's picturesque, but the truth is that it's eating at the stone like a cancer. Eventually, even the bricks have their deaths in Venice. [...]

The cold mists, rain and *acqua alta*s of autumn traditionally find us shivering and unwashed, crouching by a small electric heater, bleating into the telephone. The boiler always fails as soon as the central heating is turned on, because of the build-up of sediment. Eventually you lure a plumber to the house. But Venetian plumbers are like teenage girls. They can't do anything for more than an hour without getting bored and needing a sweet drink and to go shopping. Mentally calculating the number of bars between San Vidal and the plumbing supplies shop at San Barnaba (seven), you go back to your desk to write some more metaphors about water. You know you'll have plenty of time to work up a poetic idea before the plumber gets back.

For Venetians, late October also means time to get the water-gates resealed with fresh rubber. Last year I forgot. Then came the historic tide of December 1. The rugs, curtains, legs of antique furniture were all thoroughly marinated in filthy flood-water before I could get back to the house. The first thing I did on arriving was wade through our hall to lift the gates to let the water *out*. The water-gates had failed because the rubber had dried out and become friable. It crumbled like a macaroon at the first lick of the tide.

The spectacular high tides have their corresponding dramatic low ones. Sometimes those profound lows do a mysterious thing: suck the water out of the lavatories and replace it with primaeval stink. And the damp brings out the *scolopendre*. These scuttling, lurking, biting creatures blend all the least charming characteristics of millipedes and cockroaches. [...]

And in winter there's the problem of frozen water that inserts itself in cracks of antique stone, expands, and enlarges the fissures. The stone parapet above our balcony has become our sword of Damocles. It's now a serious danger, raining delicate stone flakes in a constant, lyrical fashion. Our neighbours know, but this building dates to 1355, and is *vincolato vincolato* – protected to the limit of the law. You cannot undertake even urgent maintenance without planning permission. We're still waiting. The flakes are still falling; bigger ones now.

Like a high-tech ancient mariner, you listen to the shrieks, not of an albatross, but of the *acqua alta* sirens. They tell you whether the tide's going to be a nuisance, a damned nuisance, a worry or a crisis (100cm, 120cm, 140cm, 155cm above the base tide respectively). You also adjust your footwear accordingly: galoshes, wellies, fisherman's thighboots. Or slippers, because there's no way you're going out in *that*.

But would I live anywhere else? An emphatic no. As a pale blue mist sighs in from the lagoon, and as the water laps gently into the hall, an egret wades along our submerged jetty on its yellow star-shaped feet.

Water is an enemy you can't help but love.

Michelle Lovric, 'Waterproofing' (2009)

A longer version of this piece was first posted as a diary piece on the English Writers in Italy website (www.englishwritersinitaly.com) in November 2009.

✳ ✳ ✳

The sirens that sounded the alarm during the air raids of the Second World War have been kept on top of the *campanili*. Now they announce sea raids, when the *acqua alta* is about to rise: they wake you at five, six in the morning. The sleepy inhabitants fix steel bulkheads to their front doors and slide little dams into the rubberised metal frames attached to their doorposts. Even the ground-floor windows facing the water-swollen canals are reinforced: more often there's really nothing to be done, the water gushes from the manhole covers, surges up through the cracks in the floor, stains the furniture, drenches the walls, ruins the paintwork. Shopkeepers dash to switch on the hydraulic pumps, frantically lift the goods from their lower shelves. Years ago, after a particularly powerful *acqua alta*, I remember improvised stalls outside the shops selling off flood-damaged shoes. Special teams of dustmen come out at dawn to set up wooden gangways in the submerged *calli*. Secondary-schoolchildren wearing knee-high rubber boots – or waders covering the whole leg – give their friends, the ones wearing ordinary shoes, a lift home; boys load the sweet cargo of a pretty classmate on to their backs; they might even give ungainly piggybacks to their teachers, arms wrapped round shoulders, hands under knees: at a distance of thirty centuries they impersonate Aeneas bringing his father Anchises to safety as they fled burning Troy. If you went out in the wrong shoes, you go into the grocer's to ask for a pair of plastic shopping bags, bag up your feet and tie the handles around your ankles. Boys with wheelbarrows ferry pedestrians across puddles big as swimming-pools and deposit them on dry land, in return for a coin. Tourists love it, take snapshots, walk about barefoot with their trousers rolled up fisherman-style, and tread on invisible underwater dog-shit; there's always one who walks blissfully on, laughing his head off and generally rejoicing, unaware that he is getting dangerously close to the edge of the submerged *fondamenta*, the invisible shore beneath his feet has come to an end, but he goes on dragging his ankles under the water until he misses his step and suddenly plunges into the canal.

Tiziano Scarpa, *Venice is a Fish* (2000)
translated by Shaun Whiteside

* * *

And a vivid description by Juan Manuel de Prada ...

'San Marco,' announced one of the crew, in order to rouse the disheartened and drowsy tourists.

Near the landing stage, two monolithic columns rose straight out of the water because the flood had taken possession of the most famous square in the world, that priceless location which, winter after winter, blends into the lagoon and threatens to surrender to it like the island of Atlantis hesitating to take the final plunge. On top of those columns reposed bronze casts of the wingèd lion of St Mark and the statue of St Theodore, ostentatious symbols of a primacy lost centuries ago. The *acqua alta* swamped the landing stage made of sagging planks and sought shelter in the Palace of the Doges, under the columned archways that form a filigree of stone. From the mooring place as far as the Mercerie a long duckboard pontoon allowed recent arrivals to keep their feet dry as they crossed that scene which the combination of snow and flood had transformed into an underwater dream world. The crew of the *vaporetto* said goodbye to us in an impenetrable language, a mixture of Venetian dialect and macaronic English, and they watched us go with a resigned and funereal compassion such as would be aroused by condemned exiles when abandoned to their fate on the beach of an island frequented only by wild beasts and mariners who have lost their bearings.

I refused to allow myself to be cast down by any sense of exclusion, in spite of the fact that the welcome extended by the drowned city did not inspire me with enthusiasm. I advanced cautiously across the pontoon; the snow cushioned my steps and scrunched beneath my feet with a sort of crackling sound, like an invertebrate animal that dares not protest as it is squashed – but snow recovers from footfalls, just as it does from blood spilled on its white surface, as, a short time later,

I should have the opportunity to confirm – and it made me sense the remorse a man must feel after violating the virginity of a young girl, or abusing an innocent person. The square of St Mark's, overrun by filth swept in by the floodwaters, had the despoiled and distressed atmosphere of a dance hall at the end of a party where the guests have drunk themselves sick, and have strewn the floor with broken bottles. The water invaded the arcades, forcing its way into the shops, spoiling the goods in the windows, and claiming right of entry into the more exclusive cafés – those with pianos and rococo mouldings, which certain cosmopolitan and literary individuals have taken it upon themselves to denigrate. The shopkeepers and waiters – the latter with a reluctance becoming their superior station – prolonged their working day mopping up, but they did so with the grudging discontent of those performing a formal duty or suffering from a biblical curse. They were the only people in the square, and their air of impassive resignation added to its desolate appearance. The sense of desolation was contagious: a sour welcome, enough to discourage any traveller from pursuing his quest. [...]

The pontoon ended suddenly when it reached the Mercerie, a labyrinth of tiny streets where a bazaar-like infinity of smart boutiques exists cheek by jowl with souvenir shops, second-hand bookshops, and banks. The pontoon ended, but the floodwaters did not, so I resigned myself to proceeding to my hotel through water made mushy by the snow melting under my feet. My trousers were wet to the knee, the tails of my raincoat were soaked, and I ruined for ever a pair of shoes not designed for paddling through rivers – even though I walked on tiptoe, trying to keep my balance as I juggled my luggage.

Juan Manuel de Prada, *The Tempest* (1997)
translated by Paul Antill

✳ ✳ ✳

According to this short extract from Jane Langton's The Thief of Venice, *not enough is being done to protect the city from the depredations of the* acqua alta.

Every day the high water was worse. The meteorologist reporting for the local TV station in the Palazzo Labia talked excitedly about the dire results of bureaucratic delay in dealing with *acqua alta*. "One!" – he held up his left hand and raised his fingers one at a time – "the delay in raising the level of the pavement in Piazza San Marco. Two! the delay in constructing mobile barriers and reinforcing the jetties at the three entrances to the lagoon. Three! the delay in completing the dredging of silt from the canals to speed up the flushing of high water. Four! the delay in preventing pollution from the passage of tankers within the island barrier. Five! The delay in preventing the discharge of pollutants from the mainland." The meteorologist gave up on his fingers as a large map appeared behind him. It was alive with arrows running northward in the Adriatic, pointing directly at the city of Venice. The arrows were the violent winds resulting from a steep drop in atmospheric pressure.

The wind was real. Homer, Mary, and Sam were blown sideways as they splashed to the San Zaccaria stop on the Riva through a retreating slop of water, and took the next vaporetto up the Grand Canal.

Jane Langton, *The Thief of Venice* (1999)

✣ ✣ ✣

And then there's the fog ... Venetian Paolo Barbaro describes its arrival.

This windless morning is heavy with the sirocco, and the great wall of damp materializes in the air as an infinity of tiny spheres, microscopic globes like infinitesimal soap bubbles. It's more a slow *sfumando*, a fading, shading, and thinning, than a typical sfumato, dissolving and nebulously refracting the rays of a white sun, motionless in its preordained place; the water, too, all rainbow bubbles and tiny, repeated, prolonged, tireless reflections until you don't understand the sense of what you're seeing. In the lagoon the weather "happens" at eleven o'clock every morning, explains Ughetto, who's been watching it for the past forty years. And he's right; every morning at eleven the wind rises, whether it's a breeze or a gale. Here and there, suddenly or little by little, the wall of bubbles, the curving crest of vapours breaks up. Or else it swells, rises, and expands. Bubbles, mist, and vapours: the daily trilogy of weather and water. It depends on the wind, the pressure, the light – and who knows what else that I can't see, and Ughetto knows but doesn't explain: "Feel it, there it is."

A brief breath from the south, and the moist clouds spanning the whole edge of the lagoon, departing from all our real or presumed S-shaped frontiers, move out to fall gently upon Venice. They drop down onto the compact aggregate of houses, the great Fish made up of canals and canal banks, islands and mirrors of water. They permeate the islands and those of us who inhabit them so that we become, not so much human beings, as fish ourselves.

It's the moment in which the cloud overtakes the city from every direction, rising up from the water and descending from the sky, swirling out in tendrils and fingers of fog, unfurling from every underground tunnel, climbing up out of the ancient wells, evaporating from the sewers and drains, stagnating on the canal banks, invading the calli, winding around the trees in the campi and flower and vegetable gardens, in Castello, Cannaregio, on the Lido, wrapping the boats and ships in a shroud, penetrating both stones and bones. It can last this intensely for days, but whether it's dense or light, it's always around; there's no escaping it.

Paolo Barbaro, *Venice Revealed* (1998)
translated by Tami Calliope

✳ ✳ ✳

*There's plenty of convincing 'literary' fog around, too
– especially in the many detective stories set in Venice.
Here's some in Donna Leon's* Death at La Fenice *and
in Michael Dibdin's* Dead Lagoon.

The next morning was as dismal as his mood. A thick fog
had appeared during the night, seeping up from the waters on
which the city was built, not drifting in from the sea. When
he stepped out of his front door, cold, misty tendrils wrapped
themselves around his face, slipped beneath his collar. He could
see clearly for only a few metres, and then vision grew cloudy;
buildings slipped into and out of sight, as though they, and
not the fog, shifted and moved. Phantoms, clothed in a nimbus
of shimmering grey, passed him on the street, floating by as
though disembodied. If he turned to follow them with his eyes,
he saw them disappear, swallowed up by the dense film that
filled the narrow streets and lay upon the waters like a curse.
Instinct and long experience told him there would be no boat
service on the Grand Canal; the fog was far too thick for that.
He walked blindly, telling his feet to lead, allowing decades of
familiarity with bridges, streets, and turns to take him over to
the Zattere and the landing where both the number 8 and the
number 5 stopped on their way to the Giudecca.

Service was limited, and the boats, divorced from any idea
of a schedule, appeared randomly out of clouds of fog, radar
screens spinning. He waited fifteen minutes before a number 5
loomed up, then slammed heavily into the dock, rocking it and
causing a few of the people waiting there to lose their balance
and fall into one another. Only the radar saw the crossing; the
humans huddled down in the cabin, blind as moles in sand.

Donna Leon, *Death at La Fenice* (1992)

✳ ✳ ✳

By morning, a dense fog had settled on the city. When a combination of high tides and strong onshore winds flooded the streets with the dread *aqua alta*, the council posted maps showing the zones affected and the routes on higher ground which remained open, but the fog respected no limits. It ebbed and flowed according to its own laws, blossoming here, thinning there, blurring outlines, abolishing distinctions and making the familiar strange and unlikely. [...]

On the Cannaregio, a slight breeze was at work, stirring the fog into currents of differing density. The palaces and churches fronting the canal came and went, the forms firming up and vagueing away like a print from an old photographic plate damaged by the ravages of time. A barge nosed through out from a side canal into the main channel, hooting mournfully. Similar sirens and signals, muffled by the moist air, resounded in the distance.

Zen was making slow progress towards the ferry stop when he was hurled headlong to the cobbles, banging his knee and shoulder painfully. Getting up again and looking round, he saw the line of tubing over which he had tripped, straight lengths of metal bolted together with blue concertina inserts in plastic to accommodate corners. Down at the quayside one of the ubiquitous red barges marked POZZI NERI would be moored ready to receive the contents of whichever septic tank was being drained that morning.

He picked up his briefcase, lit a cigarette and continued on his way across the bridge to the floating platform where a dozen people were already waiting. Spectral in the fog, the massive wooden pilings chained together to form a tripod securing the platform, their tops phallically round, looked like an idol dedicated to some god of the lagoon. From time to time invisible craft passed by, the wash making the landing stage shift restlessly at its moorings.

At length a muffled cone of light appeared in the fog, gradually brightening and widening until the boat itself became visible,

131

one of the *motoscafi* with a rakishly high bow like a torpedo boat. The waiting crowd filed on board and the ferry continued cautiously on its way, creeping through the water, the engine barely turning over, the searchlight at the bow scanning back and forth. Once they cleared the mouth of the Cannaregio the water started to heave dully, making the boat yaw and wallow.

Michael Dibdin, *Dead Lagoon* (1994)

* * *

And an 'historical' fog from Michelle Lovric's The Floating Book *– a novel on the perilous beginnings of the print industry in Venice.*

In certain light-suffused mists, Venice deconstructs herself. One sees faint smears of silhouettes, and in these the architect's early sketches: the skeletons of the *palazzo* as he saw them on paper when they were only dreams. When the haze lifts, those buildings swell again with substance, as if freshly built. But until that happens the Venetians *nose* their way around their city.

In the thickened air every stink and every fragrance is unbearably intensified. The canals smell of billy goat and grass-clippings, the ever-present steam of sea-louse soup smells of dark sea caves, the babies smell of mouse holes, and the women smell of what they desire.

When the sea vapour blanked the town in those days, the streets were dark; only the *cesendoli*, little shrines to the Madonna, remained perpetually lit, and a few lamps under the arcades until the fourth hour of the night. The unpaved streets lurched rutted and holed; the wooden bridges were prone to collapse unexpectedly, rendering the mist, already churning with possibilities of dangerous and wonderful encounters, more threatening and more exciting.

The fog swallowed noises, belching soft echoes of them. Rocking like a sleeping crib on the water, the city cocked a blind ear, sniffed like a mole. On days like that, men and women shuffled through their town like sleepwalkers, their nostrils flared, their toes splayed and all their animal senses acutely alert.

The fog created intimate pockets, making impromptu couples of people who merely passed in the street, uniting for brief moments lantern sellers, fried food hawkers, wool beaters, mask makers, fabric stretchers, caulkers. It parted to reveal instantaneous tableaux which soon disappeared again in the vapour – a fat flute player who looked like a constipated but hopeful baby puckering up his lips for the spoon; *scuole* of *battuti* – flagellants who, veiled and bare-backed, perambulated the city scourging themselves with iron chains and birch branches; a cat and her husband in the business of procreation.

Or, out of the mist might loom the face of a large, grinning pig. It was not long since the Senate had outlawed the vagrant Tantony boars that still caused havoc in the streets. The pigs, supposed to be fed by the charity of the faithful, were but loosely tended by the monks of San Antonio. The beasts had grown fat and fierce by merely helping themselves to whatever food they wanted. When the mist soused their bristles they grew skittish, knocking unsuspecting passers-by into the freezing canals.

M. R. Lovric, *The Floating Book* (2003)

❋ ❋ ❋

Then suddenly it's winter.

At last the weather broke. Ice storms and snow suddenly replaced the searing heat, as if autumn had been foresworn entirely.

At first the Venetians stood in the freezing rain, mouths open, letting the large drops crack like quails' eggs on their heads, and the water run down their throats. But the cold quickly grew unbearable and they bustled into the taverns, enjoyably lamenting the unspeakable weather, taking out all the old complaints from last winter, dusting them down, and finding them almost inadequate to describe the infidel clouds, gusts, showers and treacherous crusts of ice on the streets. Soon a robe of frozen ermine clad the town in a silence crisped with nostalgia for the former blue-and-white damask skies.

M. R. Lovric, *The Floating Book* (2003)

✳ ✳ ✳

Although not a native of the city, Joseph Brodsky (1940–1996) paid long and regular visits. In fact, he is even buried on the cemetery island of San Michele. Here is his evocation of Venice in winter.

Then, almost imperceptibly at first, but with increasing intensity, it began to snow.

Winter is an abstract season: it is low on colours, even in Italy, and big on the imperatives of cold and brief daylight. These things train your eye on the outside with an intensity greater than that of the electric bulb availing you of your own features in the evening. If this season doesn't necessarily quell your nerves, it still subordinates them to your instincts; beauty at low temperatures *is* beauty. [...]

The winter light in this city! It has the extraordinary property of enhancing your eye's power of resolution to the point of microscopic precision [...] The sky is brisk blue; the sun, escaping its golden likeness beneath the foot of San Giorgio, sashays over the countless fish scales of the *laguna*'s lapping ripples; behind you, under the colonnades of the Palazzo Ducale, a bunch of stocky fellows in fur coats are revving up *Eine Kleine Nachtmusik*, just for you, slumped in your white chair and squinting at the pigeons' maddening gambits on the chessboard of a vast *campo*. The espresso at your cup's bottom is the one black dot in, you feel, a miles-long radius. Such are the noons here. In the morning this light breasts your windowpane and, having pried your eyes open like a shell, runs ahead of you, strumming its lengthy rays – like a hot-footed schoolboy running his stick along the iron grate of a park or garden – along arcades, colonnades, red-brick chimneys, saints, and lions. [...]

Winter, when the local fog, the famous *nebbia*, renders this place more extemporal than any palace's inner sanctum, by obliterating not only reflections but everything that has a shape: buildings, people, colonnades, bridges, statues. Boat services are cancelled, airplanes neither arrive nor take off for weeks, stores are closed, and mail ceases to litter one's threshold. The effect is as though some raw hand had tuned all those enfilades inside out and wrapped the lining around the city. Left, right, up, and down swap places, and you can find your way around only if you are a native or were given a cicerone. The fog is thick, blinding, and immobile. The latter aspect, however, is of advantage to you if you go out on a short errand, say, to get a pack of cigarettes, for you can find your way back via the tunnel your body has burrowed in the fog; the tunnel is likely to stay open for half an hour. This is a time for reading, for burning electricity all day long, for going easy on self-deprecating thoughts or coffee, for listening to the BBC World Service, for going to bed early. [...]

In winter you wake up in this city, especially on Sundays, to the chiming of its innumerable bells, as though behind your gauze curtains a gigantic china teaset were vibrating on a silver tray in the pearl-grey sky. You fling the window open and the room is instantly flooded with this outer, peal-laden haze, which is part damp oxygen, part coffee and prayers. [...] On days like this, the city indeed acquires a porcelain aspect, what with all its zinc-covered cupolas resembling teapots or upturned cups, and the tilted profile of campaniles clinking like abandoned spoons and melting in the sky. Not to mention the seagulls and pigeons, now sharpening into focus, now melting into air. I should say that, good though this place is for honeymoons, I've often thought it should be tried for divorces also – both in progress and already accomplished. There is no better back-drop for rapture to fade into; whether right or wrong, no egoist can star for long in this porcelain setting by crystal water, for it steals the show. [...]

Seasons are metaphors for available continents, and winter is always somewhat antarctic, even here. The city doesn't rely on coal as much as it used to; now it's gas. The magnificent, trum-petlike chimneys resembling medieval turrets in the backdrop of every Madonna and Crucifixion idle and gradually crumble away from the local skyline. As a result you shiver and go to bed with your woollen socks on, because radiators keep their erratic cycles here even in hotels. Only alcohol can absorb the polar lightning shooting through your body as you set your foot on the marble floor, slippers or no slippers, shoes or no shoes. If you work in the evening you burn parthenons of candles – not for ambience or better light, but for their illusory warmth; or else you move to the kitchen, light the gas stove, and shut the door. Everything emanates cold, the walls especially. Windows you don't mind because you know what to expect from them. In fact, they only pass the cold through, whereas walls store it. I remember once spending the month of January in an apart-ment on the fifth floor of a house near the church of Fava. The place belonged to a descendant of none other than Ugo Foscolo. The owner was a forest engineer or some such thing, and was, naturally, away on business. The apartment wasn't that big: two rooms, sparsely furnished. The ceiling, though, was extraordinarily high and the windows were correspond-ingly tall. There were six or seven of them, as the apartment was a corner one. In the middle of the second week the heating went off. This time I was not alone, and my comrade-in-arms and I drew lots as to who would have to sleep by the wall. 'Why should I always have to go to the wall?' she'd ask beforehand. 'Because I'm a victim?' And her mustard-and-honey eyes would darken with incredulity upon losing. She would bundle up for the night – pink woollen jersey, scarf, stocking, long socks – and having counted *uno, due, tre!* jump into the bed as though it were a dark river. [...] In the end I fell ill. Cold and dampness got me – or rather my chest muscles and nerves, messed up by surgeries. The cardiac cripple in me panicked and she somehow shoved me onto the train for Paris, as we both were unsure of the local hospitals, much though I adore the façade of Giovanni e Paolo. The carriage was warm, my head was splitting from nitro pills, and a bunch of *bersaglieri* in the compartment were celebrating their home leave with Chianti and a ghetto blaster. I wasn't sure whether I would make it to Paris; but what was interfering with my fear was the clear sense that, should I manage, in no time at all – well, in a year – I'd be back ...

Joseph Brodsky, *Watermark* (1992)

❊ ❊ ❊

A wonderful description of Venice under snow in 1791 ...

In the winter of 1791, the Venetian lagoon had frozen over.

I remember the day it first started to snow. The cold slackened its clutch on us for a moment and the flakes started to float like tiny forgiving sighs from the sky. At first it lay upon the pavements and the canals, not dissolving but roaming over the glassy water like petals. But the cold crept up out of the depths of the land and sea to seize it. Soon the Grand Canal and lagoon were impacted with dark ice. Then the snow turned angry. First, it fell from the sky in great clumps like pitchforks of hay. Then it snowed more, thrice and threefold more, as if the sky hated us and wanted to bury us forever like the fabled cities enfolded in the sand-dunes of Egypt. Then it snowed bandages across the windows of the city, binding our eyes so we could see nothing but whiteness. The *palazzi* were encased in ice that rendered into dead pastels all our vivid terracottas and porphyries. Finally it snowed in a great sheet of white, like a winding-cloth for the corpse of the frozen city. Then it stopped snowing and became still as death.

M. R. Lovric, *Carnevale* (2001)

✳ ✳ ✳

More cold and snow as described by Juan Manuel de Prada in The Tempest.

January was setting in like an opiate; cold and harsh, but with a measure of serenity. The outlines of Venice were just visible in the distance beneath a protective shield of snow held in a precarious balance, which seemed to augur its destruction. A clammy mist over the lagoon clung limpet-like to the stone, blurring its contours and bestowing on the palaces lining the Grand Canal the appearance of closed and shuttered facto-ries, on which the chipped masonry of the façades resembled sores on the body of a leper. Venice possessed something of a leper who persists in remaining upright even after the verdict of dissolution has been decreed; Venice possessed something redolent of death, and nothing could conceal the onset of decay. From the streetlamps illuminating at intervals the Riva degli Schiavoni traces of light melted into the mist like the pale slime of snails while the *vaporetto* cut through the waters of the Grand Canal with a noise like the rattle of an old cart, which *vaporetti* make in winter when ice collects in the engines and makes them judder. The *vaporetto* from Marco Polo airport carried only half a dozen lonely and sleepy tourists who had given up talking to each other, thereby making their weary journey seem even longer; or possibly they were affected by that inexorable and mute dejection that characterises cities on the point of foundering – for Venice was foundering: the water of the lagoon had risen above the level of the *rive*, invading the halls of palaces and the porticoes of churches, and spreading its infestation of mud and lapping waves up to the mosaics of the Basilica of St Mark, which stood out in the background like a mammoth resigned to its fate, its foundations weakened by the damp, and its cupolas, belly upwards, breathing the corrosive night air. [...]

Then, almost imperceptibly at first, but with increasing intensity, it began to snow. It settled on the lagoon instantly, as if falling on dry land, and I watched this phenomenon, which seemed to defy the laws of physics, with the same grateful wonder with which the Jews must have received the fall of manna in the middle of their exodus: I did not know that snow fell on cities beside the sea – as a true provincial I thought that snow was the prerogative of mountain country – I did not know that snow could settle on the sea without melting. In less than five minutes, the swirl had become dense and the lagoon was carpeted with an unblemished whiteness that the *vaporetto* defiled with its bows as it made its way through it. Behind us, we left a wash of black, churning water over whose scars the snow quietly laid its blessed mantle. I had never experienced such a heavy snowstorm, never had I witnessed such a wild scene of nature, which violated its own laws and drew us into a world of unreality. It was snowing over the lagoon, it was snowing over Venice, and it was snowing on me.

Juan Manuel de Prada, *The Tempest* (1997)
translated by Paul Antill

✳ ✳ ✳

But finally spring arrives. Many would say it's the best season in Venice. Paolo Barbaro describes the wildlife of the city coming back to life and reminds us that the city's treasures are not all man made.

Spring arrives and everyone hits the streets at the first touch of sun and doesn't go home until late at night: old people, teenagers, children, workers coming and going among piles of rubble and the new fibre-optic excavations that litter the city. There are words in the wind, calls, greetings, and sounds of all kinds – Venice is coming to life. The voices of the first tourists echo from the canals and we can't even pin them down yet, can't tell where they come from. We're out of practice. And, ah – here it is, the first time this year: "*O Sole Mio*" from the gondola tour in Rio Malcanton. [A local joke at the tourists' expense: this is a Neapolitan song.] It's the usual singer, looking just a little more tired than last year. Windows are thrown open so that the city can enter the house. Venetian houses, with their many windows, seem made just for this – to let the city in – and vice versa, in a continuous exchange. Soon the mosquitoes will make themselves known. [...]

Dogs, cats, pigeons, seagulls, flies, ants, blackbirds, and sparrows are all strolling along the canal banks companionably, among the human beings. I can picture the mice, lying in wait within their holes in the banks. Life parades itself in a thousand forms. The cries of the gulls resound from the sky and water (in the streets, they're almost always silent), endlessly repeated, almost exactly alike, like the calls of certain ducks in the country marshes. Herring gulls and what we call in dialect *magoghe* and *cocài*. One lone robin, only one, since robins aren't clever; they're way too beautiful and the cats get them every time. Then there are the grebes, the *fisoli*, at the vaporetto landings, always more of them in and out of the water, even bobbing along in the vaporetto's wake. I've been told there are geckos in San Stae, sunning themselves in the courtyard. The islands are teeming with egrets and *marangoni*, a kind of cormorant that swims unbelievably well, eats prodigiously, and has branched out into the city, making itself at home on the more solitary canal banks. [...]

Columns of ants march up the marble walls, the stucco, the pipes, into the kitchen and beyond. Gorgeous grasshoppers and clumsy, drunken May beetles are everywhere. Cinches crowd the grass, big, green, and silent. Large and small crabs inhabit even the most peopled fondamente – a good sign. There are eels in the canals, and tiny fish in compact schools: swarms of silver-blue wriggles and flashes beneath the green water. Throngs of mullet, gold-silver, blue-gold, leap in the bend of the Rio della Toletta and navigate the canals beneath the Bridge of the Fists, the House of God, and the Banks of the Slavs. [...]

This year, evidently, about two hundred thousand aquatic birds have chosen to winter here, more than double the human population of Venice. Pink and white herons, great white egrets in the hundreds, thousands of grebes small and large, ten to twelve thousand teals, and over a thousand cormorants have all found a home here. Even ospreys; and who knows how many naturalists from every territory on earth, to study and observe them. I've never seen so many beasts (the birds, not the naturalists) in the lagoon. They are now considered to be of "international importance," Martino assures me, "according to the Ramsar convention" – these and all other areas where at least twenty thousand specimens winter. There are ten times that many here, practically in the city. But in Venice, and in the places around Venice, no one cares very much about the Richiamo, sighs Martino. All this beauty, life incorporated in these fascinating forms, these trees, these waters, these wonderful winged ones, these voices of birds far and near, this strange music pursuing us now, only a pace away from the city – no one cares very much about any of it. Yet this music means our whole environment, including the sea, has improved in the past few years; that it's become less polluted, more limpid, more liveable. As soon as we dump a little less filth in it, the sea lends us a hand. "*El mar xe più contento,*" the fishermen say: the sea is happier now. Still, not withstanding all that we've dumped into it over the years. These are hopeful statistics, to be taken in, to be emphasised right away – but will it last, or not? At the moment it seems so. The lagoon has been preserved over the centuries, the millenia, because we've desired it so; and that's still true today.

Paolo Barbaro, *Venice Revealed* (1998)
translated by Tami Calliope

Venetians – temporary and permanent

What is it about Venice that tries to turn even the temporary or casual visitor into a full-blown Venetian? Joseph Brodsky has a possible answer.

Venice is the sort of city where both the stranger and the native know in advance that one will be on display.

No, bipeds go ape about shopping and dressing up in Venice for reasons not exactly practical; they do so because the city, as it were, challenges them. We all harbour all sorts of misgivings about the flaws in our appearance, anatomy, about the imperfections of our very features. What one sees in this city at every step, turn, perspective, and dead end worsens complexes and insecurities. That's why one – a woman especially, but a man also – hits the stores as soon as one arrives here, and with a vengeance. The surrounding beauty is such that one instantly conceives of an incoherent animal desire to match it, to be on a par. This has nothing to do with vanity or with the natural supply of mirrors here, the main one being the very water. It is simply that the city offers bipeds a notion of visual superiority absent in their natural lairs, in their habitual surroundings. That's why furs fly here, as do suede, silk, linen, wool, and every other kind of fabric. Upon returning home, folks stare in wonderment at what they've acquired, knowing full well that there is no place in their native realm to flaunt these acquisitions without scandalising the natives.

Joseph Brodsky, *Watermark* (1992)

✳ ✳ ✳

Judith Martin provides a guest list of some of the most famous temporary Venetians.

Venice is actually proud of its previous generation of tourists. Mozart once dropped by for Carnival, and his fondest memory was of being attacked by seven women determined to spank him. This may explain why his father did not allow him to return. All the same, the city council and the tourist board put up a plaque to commemorate the two hundredth anniversary of his memorable visit. George Sand, who arrived with Alfred de Musset, is honoured with a plaque on the house where she lived after she recovered from dysentery before he did and felt well enough to run off with their Venetian doctor. Cole Porter has no plaque (yet), but his name is remembered in connection with Ca' Rezzonico, the house he rented to give parties that featured a jazzy barge floating out front, to the annoyance of his neighbours. There is a plaque on Ca' Rezzonico, but it commemorates the death of another tourist, Robert Browning, whose son, Pen, once owned the building. [...]

Other tourists whose quickie visits are thought to add to the city's interest and prestige include Erasmus, Galileo, Albrecht Dürer, Johann Wolfgang von Goethe, Stendhal, Michel de Montaigne, Charles Dickens, Alfred Lord Tennyson, Mark Twain, Honoré de Balzac, Herman Melville, Percy Bysshe Shelley, Friedrich Nietzsche, J. M. W. Turner, John Singer Sargent, William Wordsworth, Henry Wadsworth Longfellow, James Fenimore Cooper, Pierre August Renoir, Claude Monet, Marcel Proust, Edith Wharton, Rainer Maria Rilke, Pyotr Illich Tchaikovsky, Thomas Mann, Max Beerbohm, and Evelyn Waugh, right up to Dr. Seuss and Woody Allen. Full-fledged Venetophiles who honoured Venice by long stays or frequent visits include – in addition to the aforementioned [previous to the chapter from which this extract is taken] Byron, Wagner, James, Hemingway, and Pound – Petrarch, El Greco, Lady Mary Wortley Montagu, John and Euphemia Ruskin, William Dean Howells, James McNeill Whistler, Mariano Fortuny, Igor Stravinsky, and Serge Diaghilev, right on up to Elton John and Dame Edna.

Historically, Venice was a cosmopolitan city, fascinated by foreigners. True, the tourists mentioned above were all what might now be roughly classified as cultured. But Lord Byron and George Sand did not always behave in the spirit prescribed by the rules that Venice has issued for current tourists, even if they may not have disobeyed the specific ones that forbid wearing bikinis around town and picnicking inside churches.

Judith Martin, *No Vulgar Hotel* (2007)

✳ ✳ ✳

A Venetian fog prompts a brief, imagined glimpse of three famous poets visiting the city in the 1950s.

A tall, smooth window of Florian's that was reasonably well lit and not covered with a board gleamed through the patches of fog. I walked toward it and looked inside. Inside, it was 195?. On the red plush divans, around a small marble table with a kremlin of drinks and teapots on it, sat Wystan Auden, with his great love, Chester Kallman, Cecil Day Lewis and his wife, Stephen Spender and his. Wystan was telling some funny story and everybody was laughing. In the middle of the story, a well-built sailor passed by the window; Chester got up and, without so much as a "See you later," went in hot pursuit. "I looked at Wystan," Stephen told me years later. "He kept laughing, but a tear ran down his cheek." At this point, for me, the window had gone dark. King Fog rode into the piazza, reined in his stallion, and started to unfurl his white turban. His buskins were wet, so was his charivari; his cloak was studied with the dim, myopic jewels of burning lamps. He was dressed that way because he hadn't any idea what century it was, let alone which year. But then, being fog, how could he?

Joseph Brodsky, *Watermark* (1992)

✳ ✳ ✳

One of the famous frequent visitors mentioned by Judith Martin – philosopher, novelist and pioneering feminist Simone de Beauvoir – kept a diary during one of her post-war visits to the city with her equally famous companion Jean-Paul Sartre. Part of her Venice diary appears in her autobiographical Force of Circumstance. *Here are some extracts.*

Tuesday 17 June
Venice; for the tenth time, or is it the twelfth? Pleasantly familiar. 'Canal closed – work in progress.' We turned off down canals we'd never seen before, so narrow it was almost impossible to pass. Charming rooms at the Cavaletto. Sartre ordered 'three teas', and settled down to work. Festy has sent me some proofs; I went to the Piazza San Marco, but there was too much music; I made myself comfortable on the bank of the canal and corrected forty pages; now I've come back here. The sky is pale with a slight wash of pink, there is a faint murmur coming up from

the gondola moorings and the quays. I must get back to work tomorrow or I'll begin to droop and pine. [...]

Friday 20 June
I'm very pleased with my room, with the ripples of light and shade moving across the ceiling and the *battie-becco* of the gondoliers. But until this morning I've been working badly, done nothing but read, and been tired. [...]

Saturday 21 June
Yesterday, at the Correr Museum, we saw an Antonello da Messina, not particularly good, but certainly concrete proof of what Sartre had told me: that he was the link between Vivarini and Giorgione's *Tempest*, and even more definitely between Belini's first and second styles. Our tastes haven't really changed much in twenty-five years; I still experience the same astonished admiration in front of the Cosimo Turas and remember my surprise when I first came upon them years ago.

We're settling down to a rhythm here. Up at 9.30, long breakfast with the newspapers in the Piazza San Marco. Work till 2.30. A snack. Sightseeing or a museum. Work from five till nine. Dinner. A Scotch at Harry's Bar. A last Scotch at midnight on the Piazza, when it's finally free of all the musicians, the tourists, the pigeons, and despite the chairs on the café terraces regains the tragic beauty Tintoretto captured in his *Abduction of Saint Mark*. [...]

Tuesday 24 June
On Sunday afternoon we went out towards the Arsenal; there was a crowd on the Fundamenta Nuova, but no tourists; they were Italians who had come to watch the regatta. Boats, canoes, gondolas, packed with people, clustering around great posts with green decorations painted around the top. Everywhere in the green lagoon – exactly the same green as the trees – there were processions of gondolas, and gondoliers, dressed in dazzling white, bent over their poles, their buttocks modelled

just as one sees them in the pictures of Carpaccio. A few russet or purplish sails; two or three yachts in the distance. We left before the regatta began. […]

After dinner at La Fenice, where the owner insisted on taking us on a tour of the kitchen, we went to Harry's Bar. […]

Monday 30 June
We revisited Torcello and saw the Carpaccios at San Giorgio again; we went up the campanile and the bells rang out in our ears. We visited the Biennale: a very bad Braque exhibition, a very lovely one of Wols; interesting sculptures by Pevsner. And we've had some charming evenings; to avoid meeting people, we've migrated from Harry's Bar to Ciro's, where a German pianist plays lovely old tunes. […]

Tuesday 1 July
Left Venice. But first we breakfasted on the Rialto, on the Grand Canal, and read the papers.

Simone de Beauvoir, *Force of Circumstance* (1963)
translated by Richard Howard

✳ ✳ ✳

Byron was probably the most renowned nineteenth-century visitor to adopt (and be adopted by) Venice. In her novel Carnevale, *Michelle Lovric recreates the great poet's relationship with the city.*

Byron loved Venice, and soon Venice began to love him back. In him Venice had, as usual, obtained the *crème de la crème*. Venice has a great taste for allegory, and she inclines towards the East. When Byron came to Venice, it was as if Vathek himself had arrived. La Serenissima was perturbed, though as delightfully as possible. An English milord, suspected of crimes against God and the flesh, a mysterious deformed person, delicate and depraved, who secreted himself in the heart of Venice – *Che delizia!*

But there were few confirmed sightings to gratify the curiosity whipped up by the rumours. Byron's sightseeing had been accomplished discreetly, before the news of his arrival was quite out. Once his presence had become known, Byron cultivated his celebrity with rarity, knowing that to make one's self too available is to allow one's charm to evaporate. He knew that his short stature, his limp, his as yet imperfect grasp of Italian would undermine the enormity of his unknown persona. So, as the rumours of his presence spread, he hid himself, allowing carefully groomed incidents to become public. He sat in his parlour, waiting to be mythologised.

Those days the defiant remnants of the Venetian intelligentsia congregated in the salon of Countess Albrizzi. Byron, of course, was introduced, making a rare excursion abroad in the dark of the evening. At the Albrizzi *conversazione* he listened to the Venetian nobles reading aloud their refined little poems in languid voices. The men stood in one part of the room. At the other, the ladies sat in a semi-circle. This was the most elegant entertainment offered by Venice. He took his place amongst our aristocrats as a matter of course. [...]

Byron's stock only increased when a Venetian newspaper published a review of Caroline Lamb's *Glenarvon*, along with a breathless description of the attempted suicide of the noble authoress in the sad throes of her hopeless passion for the English milord. Byron made an attempt to appear livid – describing the drama to the Albrizzi guests as 'the scratching attempt at canicide of that two-handed whore'. Still, he kept the Venetian newspaper, along with another, labelling him a supporter of the hated Bonaparte. 'As curiosities,' he told me.

Byron-fever increased. His gondola was chased through the narrow canals by hooded black boats from which issued soft gusts of giggles and feminine sighs.

M. R. Lovric, *Carnevale* (2001)

✳ ✳ ✳

Joseph Kanon's Alibi *begins with another Venetophile – a woman returning to Venice after the Second World War and trying to recapture her earlier, glamorous life in the city.*

After the war, my mother took a house in Venice. She'd gone first to Paris, hoping to pick up the threads of her old life, but Paris had become grim, grumbling about shortages, even her friends worn and evasive. The city was still at war, this time with itself, and everything she'd come back for – the big flat on the Rue du Bac, the cafés, the market on the Raspail, memories all burnished after five years to a rich glow – now seemed pinched and sour, dingy under a permanent cover of grey cloud.

After two weeks she fled south. Venice at least would look the same, and it reminded her of my father, the early years when they idled away afternoons on the Lido and danced at night. In the photographs they were always tanned, sitting on beach chairs in front of striped changing huts, clowning with friends, everyone in caftans or bulky one-piece woollen bathing suits. Cole Porter had been there, writing patter songs, and since my mother knew Linda, there were a lot of evenings drinking around the piano, that summer when they'd just married. When her train from Paris finally crossed over the lagoon, the sun was so bright on the water that for a few dazzling minutes it actually seemed to be that first summer. Bertie, another figure in the Lido pictures, met her at the station in a motorboat, and as they swung down the Grand Canal, the sun so bright, the palazzos as glorious as ever, the whole improbable city just the same after all these years, she thought she might be happy again.

A week later, with Bertie negotiating in Italian, she leased three floors of a house on the far side of Dorsoduro that once belonged to the Ventimiglia family and was still called Ca' Venti. The current owner, whom she would later refer to, with no evidence, as the marchesa, took clothes, some silver-framed family photographs, and my mother's cheque and moved to the former servants' quarters on the top floor. The rest of the house was sparsely furnished, as if the marchesa had been selling it off piece by piece, but the piano nobile, all damask and chandeliers, had survived intact, and Bertie made a lend-lease of some modern furniture from his palazzo on the Grand Canal to fill a sitting room at the back. The great feature was the light, pouring in from windows that looked out past the Zattere to the Giudecca. There were maids, who came with the house without seeming to live there, a boat moored on the canal, and a dining room with a painted ceiling that Bertie said was scuola di Tiepolo but not Tiepolo himself. The expatriate community had begun to come back, opening shuttered houses and planning parties. Coffee and sugar were hard to get, but wine was cheap and the daily catch still glistened and flopped on the market tables of the pescaria. La Fenice was open. Mimi Mortimer had arrived from New York and was promising to give a ball. Above all, the city was still beautiful, every turn of a corner a painting, the water a soft pastel in the early evening, before the lamps came on. Then the music started at Florian's and the boats rocked gently at the edge of the piazzetta, and it all seemed timeless, lovely, as if the war had never happened.

Joseph Kanon, *Alibi* (2005)

✳ ✳ ✳

By contrast, a memoir of student life in the city during the 1960s, from writer and translator Amanda Hopkinson.

We never really got a grip on her very long name. She was just the Contessa di, and her exceedingly smart apartments, furnished entirely with antiques (on the principle that antiques can never clash, they came from all over the world) were on the lagoon side of St Mark's Square, over an exceedingly smart optician's. Sarah and I were two second-year History students on a term abroad. It was the optician's shop – rather than

Sarah's sudden fits of giggles that caused her to snort into the soup, or my muddle over working outward-in with the heavily embossed dinner cutlery that led to my piercing an apparently priceless Bokhara rug with a falling steak knife – that would prove our downfall.

It was just before the start of our term abroad, supposedly studying l'Arte del Rinascimento, in one of the few Italian cities that did not display it, and which functioned mainly as a prompt to spend our weekends hitch-hiking through Tuscany. Sarah and I spoke no more Italian than that afforded by a crash course in a language lab, and my then boyfriend, who had no Italian at all, was spending a few autumnal days there with Sarah and myself. While our long dresses blended with the floral tapestries and swagged curtains within the hallowed halls of the Contessa di's apartments, Tim's more overtly hippy wear got him excluded immediately. The Contessa di told us in the plainest High Italian, *alto voce* and without a trace of Venetian dialect, lest there be the least scope for a misunderstanding, that the bed and board was for two *signorine* with no hint of a *signore*: indeed we were virtually given to understand that no member of the opposite gender had crossed her threshold since the demise of her esteemed *marito*. Tim was obliged to deposit us outside the embossed mahogany front door, and migrate downstairs, where he was told a repair could be effected on his broken glasses, inside a quarter of an hour. Various quarter hours went by, and the glasses were neither mended nor returned. Bored and hot with myopically peering at the gloomy quartet endlessly serenading scant numbers of visiting Viennese in Café Florian, Tim took up occupation of one of the white leather sofas the optician had placed in his showroom. Another couple of quarter hours went by, during which he felt increasingly unwelcome, and as unattended to as his glasses. Tim emerged onto a side alley, which he roamed ferociously until he sniffed out a vintners. Having bought a litre of the cheapest unlabelled table wine, he resumed white sofa occupation, before tugging the cork from the bottle with his teeth. He had only to raise the garnet liquid to his lips – just the faintest concealed threat his hand might jog and bring white leather disaster in its wake – for three suddenly alerted assistants to rush towards him. One seized the bottle and two seized him. The pair of spectacles was roughly inserted into his shirt pocket as he was escorted, nay ejected, through the glass doors and onto the street. Tim may have had his glasses repaired for free, but it cost Sarah and I our room in the grandest apartment we would ever visit. *Vale* to panelled walls; low-slung Murano chandeliers; gilded mirrors; portraits of centuries-deceased ancestors; and silver service with every meal in the sepulchral gloom of permanently drawn curtains. *Salve* instead to a very different square, San Giocomo dell'Orio, lined by plane trees and played in by rushing children, over by the train station. There we shared a whitewashed room with iron bedsteads and no curtains in a hostel above a bar, and the smoke of *Capitani* drifted upwards to full-blast Pavarotti skipping through *La Donna e Mobile* and the Stones belting out *Honky Tonk Women*. We braved the bar on the first evening, and were immediately adopted by a largely elderly clientele, men who worked on the boats and the railway, whose wives often worked on the canal-side market, summoned home for supper by their children. Invited by two young fishermen to join them on a midnight trawl across the moonlit lagoon, Sarah and I simultaneously reminded one another of the Contessa di's imprecations against the male gender in general, and *i Veneti* in particular. However the prospect of such a scenic setting prevailed, and we agreed to go on condition that *la nonna*, hitherto parked in the corner nearest the jukebox, so deaf that nothing interfered with her constant crocheting, came too. Much huffing and muttered imprecations (hers) ensued to shuffle the black-clad old lady down to the rowboat, and install her in the stern. Two hours of aimless drifting later, as the fish-ermen proved incapable of keeping their oars in the rowlocks, *la nonna* at least delivered. Stuffing her crochet into one side of her corsetry she extracted – to our complete astonishment – a warm package from the other. In it was a mess of polenta which, if Sarah and I could not quite bring ourselves to eat it, afforded much food for humour. The boy students gave up pretending to be gondoliers and fell upon the food, and Sarah and I rowed us back to moorings under the bridge once more. An operetta of disguised identities and old witchery, *Una Notte Veneziana*, no less.

Amanda Hopkinson, 'A Student in Venice', (2010)

❖ ❖ ❖

In this extract from John Berendt's City of Falling Angels, *a temporary Venetian observes, from his window, the lives of the local inhabitants.*

Quite apart from the twice-daily tidal rise and fall of the Miser-icordia Canal, life outside my window had a special rhythm of its own. Typically the day began in the pre-dawn still-ness when a fruit-and-vegetable dealer stepped into his boat, moored opposite my window, gently started his motor, and chugged slowly and quietly down the canal – the equivalent, for a motorboat, of tiptoeing. Then everything fell silent again, except for the lapping of water against the stones.

At about eight o'clock, life along the canal officially awoke, as shopkeepers on the other side started opening their doors and rolling up their metal gates. Giorgio set his tables and chairs out in front of the trattoria. The butcher took delivery of meat from a passing barge.

Pedestrians began moving across my field of vision like actors crossing a stage: a labourer shambling unhurriedly, a man in a business suit walking at a more purposeful pace. Customers stopped in at the trattoria for coffee and a glance at the morning's *Gazzettino*. Next door, at the local Communists' shopfront headquarters, with posters bearing the hammer-and-sickle insignia on the walls, there were generally one or two people sitting at a desk, talking on the phone or reading a newspaper. The small shop next to that one had been the work-shop of Renato Bonà, one of the last Venetian craftsmen who specialized in making oars and oar posts for gondolas. Bonà's genius as a sculptor – particularly his mastery of the curving, twisting oar posts – had made him a demigod among gondo-liers. Since his death two years earlier, his shop had become something of a shrine, commemorated by a plaque next to the door. The Misericordia Canal was not on any of the usual gondola routes, but every so often a gondola would glide by in silent tribute to Bonà. One gondola, however, had its regular mooring spot in front of the house. It was a wedding gondola, so it had elaborate carving and ornamentation, but it was still black like all the others. At some point during the day, the gondolier would ready it for a wedding by putting gold-and-white slipcovers over the chairs and cushions.

At one o'clock, the rolling of metal gates sounded again as the shops closed for midday. Only the trattoria stayed open, serving local seafood specialities to a predominantly local clientele. The pace of life slowed until late afternoon, when the shops reopened and people walked at a quickened step: students released from class, housewives hurriedly shopping for dinner.

As darkness fell, the metal gates rolled down again, and the lights of the trattoria came up at centre stage. People moved now at a leisurely stroll, and convivial voices floated in the night-time air. Towards midnight, the sounds of boats and backwash died down. The voices drifted away. Giorgio dragged the chairs and tables back inside and turned off the lights. By that time, the fruit-and-vegetable dealer had long since tethered his boat to its mooring poles, and Pino, the owner of the white water taxi, had pulled a canvas sheet over the open part of his deck and retired to his apartment above the Communists.

John Berendt, City of Falling Angels (2005)

✳ ✳ ✳

Another visitor observing the local population can't help feeling the 'unreality' of it all ... but, neverthe-less, plunges into the morning bustle of the summer-time city.

It was already desert-hot outside, but what did it matter? He was in Venice, happy to be alive, happy to be on the lookout for Laura, glad to be in Venice – which was already up and running and probably had been for hours. Fruit and veg were being sold from barges, or whatever they were called, a few gondoliers were punting for business along the canals. People were looking out of windows, shouting and waving. Barrows of produce were being wheeled through the narrow streets. It was like being in *The Truman Show*. Every day, for hundreds of years, Venice had woken up and put on this guise of being a real place even though everyone knew it existed only for tour-ists. The difference, the novelty, of Venice was that the gondo-liers and fruit-sellers and bakers were all tourists too, enjoying an infinitely extended city-break. The gondoliers enjoyed the fruit-sellers, the fruit-sellers enjoyed the gondoliers and bakers, and all of them together enjoyed the real residents: the hordes of camera-toting Japanese, the honey-mooning Americans, the euro-pinching backpackers and hungover Biennale-goers.

One of whom was walking aimlessly but with great purpose, looking for a café where he could get exactly the breakfast he wanted and to which he could return every day. [...]

He found such a place quickly, on a tiny square, with a view, at the end of a long, tree-ornamented street, of the Giudecca Canal. The coffee was sensational and by hooking out the honey – which he hated – he was able to turn the cornetto into

156

a tolerable croissant. Someone had left a copy of *La Repubblica*, which he sort of read. The big news, understandably, was the heat. *Che caldissimo!* Only nine-thirty and already it was as hot as noon.

Geoff Dyer, *Jeff in Venice, Death in Varanasi* (2009)

✳ ✳ ✳

And what about the locals' views of the visitors? One can only hope that the following isn't typical. But perhaps one should take the hint about how not *to behave as a tourist in Venice …*

As it irrupted into the lagoon after leaving the Arsenal Bridge, the *vaporetto* described a broad arc, like the first flourish a torero makes with his cape to excite the applause of a public hungering for sensation. There were a few early tourists on board who were anticipating the beginning of carnival by wearing silly hats topped with little bells. They looked, and sounded, very pleased with themselves, and failed to understand the insults that Tedeschi hurled at them in his broad Venetian dialect. As he accompanied his insults with exaggerated gestures, the tourists assumed he was welcoming them to Venice, and they responded by bowing obsequiously, making the little bells on their hats ring as they did so.

'Look at that bunch of mental defectives. You'd think somebody had shoved hot chillies up their arses … ' He laughed, showing his teeth which were as rapacious as ever, and which looked dull beside those of the grinning Japanese. 'Fucking imbeciles!'

The air over the lagoon was cold and salty. It brushed my cheeks with such a refreshing sensation that I was overwhelmed by a feeling of intense joy and […] for the first time I felt able to laugh at Tedeschi's xenophobic broadsides.

Juan Manuel de Prada, *The Tempest* (1997)
translated by Paul Antill

✳ ✳ ✳

By contrast, the charm, warmth, and generosity towards visitors exhibited by a Venetian café owner and his wife are commemorated here by novelist Michelle Lovric.

In the twelve years' I'd known him, I'd never seen Emilio's legs.

His superb big face squeezed up in greeting, yes. His teddy-bear torso drum-tight under his apron, every day. His colossal hands hovering like a priest's, yes, every morning. But his legs – no, never.

Emilio's post is behind the bar at his sparkling Gaggia, one eye on the suspended television screen, just in case something resembling a ball hoves into view. The entire bar da Gino is decorated in the patriotic *azzuro*, the walls studded with football memorabilia. His staff wear uniforms in the same colours.

Emilio's wife Graziella serves. She is shy, slight and strawberry-blonde, with a ladylike delicacy that belies her brutal working hours. The Scarpa family live on *terrafirma*. Their day starts at 4am. Six days a week, the bar opens at 6am and closes around 8pm. Then the family Scarpa cleans it lovingly, and makes the long journey home by foot, *vaporetto*, bus and foot again.

'*Un bel cappuccino per la Michelle,*' rumbles Emilio from the depths of his big blue heart. Emilio Scarpa prides himself on knowing the preferences of all his regulars. *La Michelle* likes a *cappuccino con poca schiuma* – a flat coffee nestling under a light down of dove-coloured foam calligraphed in Emilio's signature burnt-umber arabesque swirl.

The following has been tested: an informed stranger may come to Emilio's bar and ask for a '*cappuccino tipo Michelle,*' and get same. [...]

Only the tourists go to Gino's simply for the coffee, and utterly missing most of the point of the place. Like any proper

Italian bar, da Gino dispenses a stronger sustenance. It's not just Graziella's nutritious smile, or Fabrizio's serious concern for every little thing. In the breaks between rabid over-writing and savage cutting, I've made friendships at my aluminium table that have been broken only by death. Like my friend Angelo the retired gondolier (*un espresso*) who used to arrive at 6am with a small packet of birdseed and an endless supply of seduction-flavoured chat. Every morning we used to share a dozen cigarettes (him actively, me passively) and coffee.

One morning I came rushing in to Gino's, drenched, from one of Venice's apocalyptic electrical storms.

I gasped, 'The builders' crane at San Vidal got struck by lightning!'

Angelo looked blank and insisted that he had never seen the crane.

'But you must have,' I protested, 'It's huge! It's just over the Accademia Bridge. You can almost see it from here.'

He answered: '*Ma Michelle, io non guardo mai sopra perché le donne non volano,*'– 'I never look up, because women don't fly.'

He used to ask me about what kind of novel I was writing: he'd give me two alternatives to choose from, with all the appropriate gestures: either 'kiss-kiss' or 'boom-boom' (pistol shots). I had to say that there was more kiss-kiss than boom-boom in my novels and this seemed to please Angelo quite a lot. I still miss him, and his box of canary-feed, and even those damnable cigarettes. He'd frequently told me that he wanted to go to hell when he died, because all the interesting women – Sophia Loren, Claudia Cardinale & co – would be down there, and better still, he'd grin, '*completamente nude!*' because their clothes would have been burnt off in Purgatory.

We had another loss this year. Bart and Marilyn (*un cappuccino – ma caldo caldo*) were of that breed of sophisticated, urbane Americans who still adorn Venice like Henry James in his time. Bart and Marilyn were Gino's stalwarts, breakfasting there all summer. In the winter I emailed them Gino-bulletins: about Valentina's twins, about Fabrizio's daughter, about the night Italy won the world cup and Emilio nearly died of joy.

Bart died in January. Marilyn had no appetite for life without him and dwindled, losing nothing of her Southern grace, until she too was gone. I wrote to Emilio and Graziella to tell them the sad news: for a little while I could not bear to go to Gino's, because I knew I would cry when I saw them. Then I realized how stupid that was. I went. And I cried. And it was good.

Marilyn had instructed that some of her ashes were to be scattered in Venice. Her daughter brought them from New York. We knelt at our jetty scattering them in the Grand Canal along with the petals of two dozen peach-coloured roses. It was an ebb tide. A few minutes later the petals, and Marilyn, would have been passing by Gino's.

Then I took Marilyn's daughter to meet Emilio and Graziella, whose hospitality had meant so much to her parents.

And that was how I came to see Emilio's legs. I'd told him the day before of our plans. On seeing us arrive with our stricken faces and a girl who was a young facsimile of his beloved and now departed customer, Emilio turned down the lever of the Gaggia, wiped his hands on his apron, *and came out from behind the bar.*

He took the hand of Marilyn's daughter and, with me translating, for ten minutes told her the most beautiful things she had ever heard about her mother.

Then he wiped his eyes and went back behind the bar and executed three flawless *cappuccini tipo Michelle.*

Michelle Lovric, 'Emilio's legs' (2010)

✳ ✳ ✳

But what's it like to be a born-and-bred Venetian?
Michael Dibdin's Inspector Aurelio Zen finds himself

> *contemplating a group of Venetian schoolchildren on
> a rush-hour boat across the Lagoon.*

As they passed the modernistic council houses on San Girolamo and emerged into the open waters of the lagoon, the full strength of the wind became clear for the first time. The boat banged and buffeted its way through the short, hard waves, swathes of spray drenching the decking and the windows of the helmsman's cabin. Zen's cigarette obliged him to stand outside, at the top of the stairs leading down to the saloon. It was rush hour, and the boat was packed with schoolchildren and commuters. They sat or stood impassively, reading papers, talking together or staring blankly out of the windows. Apart from the pitching and rolling, the crunch of the waves and the draughts of air laden with salt, not fumes, it might almost have been the bus which Zen took to work every morning in Rome. He eyed the children hunched under their satchels, chattering brightly or horsing about. They thought this was normal, he reflected, as he once had. They thought everywhere was like this.

Michael Dibdin, Dead Lagoon (1994)

✻ ✻ ✻

> *Venice may be exquisite to the eyes of the visitor, but
> it isn't an easy place to live in for the average Vene-
> tian. Two short passages highlight the difficulties.*

Because of the scarcity of space, people exist here in cellular proximity to one another, and life evolves with the immanent logic of gossip. One's territorial imperative in this city is circumscribed by water; the window shutters bar not so much daylight or noise (which is minimal here) as what may emanate from inside. When they are opened, shutters resemble the wings of angels prying into someone's sordid affairs, and like the spacing of statues on cornices, human interplay here takes on the aspects of jewellery or, better yet, filigree. In these parts one is both more secretive and better informed than the

161

police in tyrannies. No sooner do you cross the threshold of your apartment, especially in winter, than you fall prey to every conceivable surmise, fantasy, rumour. If you've got company, the next day at the grocery or newsagent you may meet a stare of biblical probing unfathomable, you would think, in a Catholic country. If you sue someone here, or vice versa, you must hire a lawyer on the outside. A traveller, of course, enjoys this sort of thing; the native doesn't. What a painter sketches, or an amateur photographs, is no fun for the citizen.

Joseph Brodsky, *Watermark* (1992)

✻ ✻ ✻

Faced with a high cost of living and severely limited occupational opportunity, the sparse native population keeps drifting off to the mainland. Even the rich rapidly become house-poor, thanks to the eternal struggle between their ancient properties and the daily elements. Many family residences have been sold to hotel chains or other corporations, or to mostly absentee Venetophiles from a species formerly known as American Millionaires, but now called Industrialists from Milan. In others, the owners may seal off dozens of rooms to live in the few that they can afford to heat, or use their aristocratic titles and heirlooms to peddle themselves as "hosts" to the tourist trade.

Judith Martin, *No Vulgar Hotel* (2007)

✻ ✻ ✻

A young visitor notices there's one 'cultural activity' that is minimal in Venice ... and also comments on some connected gender issues in Italy as a whole.

We cross the little canal from Campo Santa Margherita over into Campo San Barnaba, then walk to Accademia past the Toletta bookshops – novels, art, design and architecture books, all themselves wonderfully designed and piled high in the window. And inside the shops? Completely empty. Not a single customer. Thinking about it, I've seen very few people reading in Venice. Something about the city seems to draw one away from intellectual labour of any kind. It seems wrong to shun the view in order to stare at a printed page instead.

'It's shaming,' I say to Ginevra as we look in. 'Look how many books there are in translation. And you can see they've spent time making them look good. In England we don't have that. Very few foreign writers are read in translation.'

Ginevra nods and gives the lonely, misunderstood sigh of the long-term bookworm. Before we move on I notice something depressing. In the Italian literature section there are about forty books on display, stacked tight along the glass. Not one by a woman. And that morning, when I was reading the newspaper Stef's parents get, there were no women journalists, no women on the list of staff writers and no women mentioned in any article. Every news photograph was of a smiling man in a suit surrounded by other smiling men in suits. I wonder at the gallantry I've witnessed over the past few days – wonder if it's merely the surface reward for women's actual exclusion.

Bidisha, *Venetian Masters* (2008)

✳ ✳ ✳

You can hardly miss one distinct group of Venetians – the musicians who play outside the cafés around St Mark's Square. Kazuo Ishiguro let's one of them give a glimpse of what it's like.

It was our third time playing the *Godfather* theme since lunch, so I was looking around at the tourists seated across the piazza to see how many of them might have been there the last time we'd played it. People don't mind hearing a favourite more than once, but you can't have it happen too often or they start suspecting you don't have a decent repertoire. At this time of year, it's usually okay to repeat numbers. The first hint of an autumn wind and the ridiculous price of a coffee ensure a pretty steady turnover of customers. Anyway, that's why I was studying the faces in the piazza and that's how I spotted Tibor.

He was waving his arm and I thought at first he was waving to us, but then I realised he was trying to attract a waiter. He looked older, and he'd put on some weight, but he wasn't hard to recognise. I gave Fabian, on accordion right next to me, a little nudge and nodded towards the young man, though I couldn't take either hand off my saxophone just then to point him out properly. That was when it came home to me, looking around the band, that apart from me and Fabian, there was no one left in our line-up from that summer we'd met Tibor.

Okay, that was all of seven years ago, but it was still a shock. Playing together every day like this, you come to think of the band as a kind of family, the other members as your brothers. And if every now and then someone moves on, you want to think he'll always stay in touch, sending back postcards from Venice or London or wherever he's got to, maybe a Polaroid of the band he's in now – just like he's writing home to his old village. So a moment like that comes as an unwelcome reminder of how quickly things change. How the bosom pals of today become lost strangers tomorrow, scattered across Europe, playing the *Godfather* theme or 'Autumn Leaves' in squares and cafés you'll never visit.

Kazuo Ishiguro, "Cellists" from *Nocturnes* (2009)

❉ ❉ ❉

And famous Venetians? Jan Morris encounters one …
though a little late in his career.

I saw a dead Pope once, and he was refulgent even in corpse-hood. Pius X had been Patriarch of Venice before his ascension, and when I was living in that city in 1959 he paid a posthumous revisit to his old patriarchate. We watched his passing from our balcony over the Grand Canal. Embalmed though he was by then, he moved by with infinite condescension. Gondolas full of priests came first, cushioned deep in their seats and rowed by white-robed gondoliers. Then came a series of dream-like barges, their velvet draperies trailing in the water behind. And finally in a blaze of gold came the Bucintoro, successor to the magnificent State barge of the doges of Venice, rowed by a crew of tough young sailors to the beat of a drum. Bells rang, plainchants sounded from loudpeakers across the city, and to the solemn boom, boom of the drum the cadaver of the Holy Father, flat on his back in a crystal coffin, sailed by as to the manner dead.

Jan Morris, *Europe: An Intimate Journey* (2006)

❊ ❊ ❊

The dramatist Carlo Goldoni (1707–93) is one of the city's most treasured sons. Look out for his statue.

Ten minutes later, he walked out from the *sottoportico* of Calle della Bissa and into Campo San Bartolomeo. His eyes went up to the bronze statue of Goldoni, perhaps not his favourite playwright, but certainly the one who could make him laugh the hardest, especially when the plays were presented in their original Veneziano dialect, as they always were here, in the city that swarmed to his plays and loved him enough to put up this statue. Goldoni was in full stride, which made this *campo* the perfect place for him to be, for here, everyone rushes, always on their way somewhere: across the Rialto Bridge to go to the vegetable market; from Rialto to either the San Marco or the Cannaregio district. If people lived anywhere near the heart of the city, its geography would pull them through San Bartolomeo at least once a day.

Donna Leon, *The Anonymous Venetian* (1994)

❊ ❊ ❊

Then the lights began to come on, destroying the delicate melting equipoise of slate and rose on the water; lanterns on the marking poles out in the canal, the triple-headed street lights along the *fondamenta*, the prow lamps of gondolas.

It was half dark when he left the restaurant. He crossed the bridge again and lingered for a while in the Campo San Bartolomeo in front of the statue of Goldoni. There was a pigeon on the playwright's jaunty tricorn hat and another on his shoulder. Through the gathering darkness he looked down, Venice's favourite son, streaked with pigeon droppings, blackened by corrosion, the genial cynicism of his expression still showing through. Humorous, indulgent, gregarious ...

Barry Unsworth, Stone Virgin (1985)

❉ ❉ ❉

Probably the most famous Venetian of them all, Giacomo Casanova (1725–98), wrote a vivid account of his adventures, amorous and otherwise. In this extract from his memoirs he finds himself in very serious trouble with the Venetian authorities.

Leaving my room, I was surprised to see thirty or forty guards in the drawing room. I was honoured they had thought so many necessary to secure my person. [...]

Messer Grande ordered me into the gondola and sat down beside me, retaining but four men and sending the rest away. Once at his headquarters, he shut me into a room after offering me coffee, which I refused. I spent four hours sleeping there, waking up every fifteen minutes to pass water. This was a strange phenomenon, for I had never suffered from strangury; the heat was excessive and I had not eaten, but in spite of this I filled two large chamber pots with urine. I had noted on other occasions that the shock of an oppressive experience had a strong narcotic effect on me, but not until now did I learn how diuretic it could be. [...]

At the sounding of the Terza bell [one of the bells of the San Marco campanile, that called the magistrates to meet], the chief guard entered the room and informed me that he had orders to put me *under the Leads* [the prisons located under the roof of the Ducal palace, which was covered with sheets of lead]. I followed him. We climbed into another gondola and, after a long detour by way of the small canals, we entered the Grand Canal and disembarked at the Quay of the Prisons. After climbing several flights of stairs, we crossed an elevated, enclosed bridge [the Bridge of Sighs] connecting the prisons to the Ducal Palace above the canal called *Rio di Palazzo*. Past this bridge, we went through a large hall, entered one room, then another, where he introduced me to a man dressed as a patrician, who after looking me over told him:

"*È quello; mettetelo in deposito.*" [He's the one, lock him up.]

But Casanova does not intend to go the way of others locked up in the infamous Venetian prison. Always resourceful and determined, he attempts – along with a fellow prisoner – a somewhat tricky escape …

I was the first to go out; Father Balbi followed after me. I told Soradaci to put the lead plate back as it was, then sent him off to pray to St. Francis. Staying down on hands and knees, I grasped my spike and, reaching forward, pushed it obliquely into the gaps between one plate and the next. In this way, by raising each plate and then grabbing onto its edge with my fingers, I was able to climb to the top of the roof. To follow behind me, the monk hooked his fingers into the belt of my breeches, near the buckle; thus I suffered the unfortunate fate of the beast that must bear a load and drag another, all the while climbing an incline made slippery by fog.

Halfway up this perilous ascent, the monk told me to stop, for one of his bundles had come unfastened from his neck and rolled back down the roof, perhaps no farther than the gutter.

My first temptation was to deal him a swift kick that would have sent him to rejoin his bundle in a hurry. But GOD gave me the strength to forbear; the punishment would have been too great for both of us, for I could never have escaped all by myself. I asked him if it was the bundle of ropes. He said it was the one with his black frock coat, two shirts and a precious manuscript he had found in the prison, which he claimed would make him rich. I calmly told him he would have to do patiently without it, for we must forge on. He sighed and, still hanging onto my rear, followed behind me.

After scaling over fifteen or sixteen lead plates, I found myself at the roof's highest point, where I spread my legs and comfortably straddled the centre ridge. The monk did likewise behind me. To our backs lay the little isle of San Giorgio Maggiore, while about a hundred paces in front of us loomed the many domes of San Marco, which form part of the Ducal palace. It is the Doge's chapel; no monarch on earth can boast of anything similar. I quickly relieved myself of my burdens and told my companion to do the same. He wedged his bundle of ropes securely between his thighs, but his hat, which he likewise wanted to put there, lost its balance and, after bounding and somersaulting down to the gutter, fell into the canal. [...]

After spending several minutes looking around to the right and left, I told the monk to stay there with the bundles and not move until I returned. I left our spot with only my spike in hand, travelling on my buttocks without difficulty, still straddling the summit of the roof. I spent nearly an hour going everywhere, looking, observing, examining; and after finding nothing, along the edges, to which I might fasten one end of my rope to lower myself to a spot where I would be safe, I was greatly perplexed. The canal and the palace courtyard were both out of the question. The upper part of the church offered only sheer drops between its domes, none of which led to a space that was not enclosed. In order to go beyond the church towards the Canonica [the houses of the Canons of San Marco], I would have had to climb over curved, steep inclines. It was natural that I should discard as impossible anything that I could not conceive to be feasible. I needed to be bold but not foolhardy. It is a middle point unknown, I believe, to morality, the most imperceptible.

My eyes and thoughts came to rest on a dormer, on the side of the Rio de Palazzo, about two-thirds of the way down the slope. It was far enough from the hole I had come out of to assure me that the garret it illuminated did not form part of the prison enclosure from which I had broken out. It could only give onto some attic, inhabited or uninhabited, above some palace apartment whose doors would naturally be opened at the beginning of the day. I was absolutely certain that any servants of the palace or of the Doge's family, should they see us, would be anxious to lead us out, and would do everything they could except put us back into the hands of the Inquisitors, even should they recognise us as the greatest criminals of the state.

Giacomo Casanova, *The Story of My Life* (1822)
translated by Stephen Sartarelli and Sophie Hawkes

✳ ✳ ✳

One event which brought together temporary Venetians and local residents alike was the destruction, by fire, of the much-loved and aptly named La Fenice (The Phoenix) opera house. Everyone from Pavorotti to Woody Allen and some 'local ladies' raised funds to help the exquisite theatre rise again from the ashes.

There had been an outpouring of sympathy for Venice. The opera singer Luciano Pavarotti had announced he would give a concert to help raise funds to rebuild the Fenice. Plácido Domingo, not to be outdone, said he would also give a concert, but *his* concert would be in St Mark's Basilica. Pavarotti shot back that he, too, would sing in St Mark's, and that he would sing there *alone*. Woody Allen, whose jazz band was to have reopened the newly renovated Fenice with a concert at the end of the month, quipped to a reporter that the fire must have been set by 'a lover of good music', adding, 'If they didn't want me to play, all they had to do was say so.'

The destruction of the Fenice was an especially brutal loss for Venice. It had been one of the few cultural attractions that had not been ceded to outsiders. Venetians always outnumbered tourists at the Fenice, so all Venetians felt a special affection for it, even those who had never set foot inside the place. The city's prostitutes took up a collection and presented Mayor Cacciari with a cheque for $1,500.

John Berendt, *City of Falling Angels* (2005)

Art and entertainment

Venice offers a wealth of art, from the first European masters to the world's most contemporary artists exhibiting at the Biennale. Goethe offers a brief but valuable insight into some early Venetian painters.

As I glided over the lagoons in the brilliant sunshine and saw the gondoliers in their colourful costume, gracefully posed against the blue sky as they rowed with easy strokes across the light green surface of the water, I felt I was looking at the latest and best painting of the Venetian school. The sunshine raised the local colours to a dazzling glare and even the parts in shadow were so light that they could have served pretty well as sources of light. The same could be said of the reflections in the water. Everything was painted clearly on a clear background. It only needed the sparkle of a white-crested wave to put the dot on the *i*.

Both Titian and Veronese possessed this clarity to the highest degree, and when we do not find it in their works, this means that the picture has suffered damage or been retouched.

Johann Wolfgang von Goethe, *Italian Journey* (1786–1788)
translated by W. H. Auden and Elizabeth Mayer

✳ ✳ ✳

In Vikram Seth's An Equal Music, *we accompany the main characters as they view a remarkable series of paintings by the fifteenth-century artist Carpaccio.*

We walk over to the Scuola. It is not crowded. Julia tells me the name of the artist whose work she has brought me to see: Carpaccio. My eyes get used to the dimness, and as they do, my mouth opens in astonishment. The paintings against the dark woodwork of the walls are the most striking I have ever seen. We stand together at the first one: a repellent dragon, attacked by St George, squirms balefully, the point of the spear breaking through its mouth and skull. A plantless wasteland of decay stretches all around. It is filled with loathesome objects – snakes, toads, lizards, heads, limbs, bones, skulls, cadavers. The foreshortened torso of a man, who looks a bit like the curly-headed St George himself might have looked had he been a victim of the dragon, stares out of the picture, one arm and one leg consumed. A maiden, half eaten from below, contrives somehow to continue to look virtuous. Everything is pallid and grotesque; yet far behind this withered tree and this fatal desert is a zone of serene beauty: a scene of ships and water, tall trees, opulent buildings.

We move from scene to scene along the wall, not speaking, one painting away from each other. I trail behind with the guidebook. The tamed, shrunken dragon awaits the final stroke of its victor's sword; pagan monarchs are spectacularly converted, while a small red parrot looks out of the painting with a cynical, speculative gaze as he nibbles the leaf of a small plant; a child is exorcised of a bizarre basilisk; across the altar on the other wall, the mild St Jerome travels about with his still milder lion, sending timorous monks fleeing like cloned bats across the canvas; the little red parrot appears again as St Jerome piously dies; and then, most wondrous of all, the news of his death appears to St Augustine in his rich, calm study, lined with books, adorned with open music, where he sits alone with his gorgeous, impeccable, polite, adoring, curly-haired white dog, than which there is nothing more perfect or more necessary in this room, or in Venice, or the world.

Vikram Seth, *An Equal Music* (1999)

✻ ✻ ✻

For the lover of modern art, Venice offers not only the Biennale but the wonderful museum created by American art-lover Peggy Guggenheim. Eva Demski tells us about it.

Time and time again famous people and those less famous have ended up in Venice and attempted to become locals – and it doesn't work, of course. Instead, the city cunningly turns them into attractions in their own right: without realizing it, they become circus horses, fire-swallowers, and contortionists.

On the Grand Canal, there is something that looks like a palace with the top sliced off. Every art enthusiast knows this odd unfinished building, flat and strange to look at, lying there like a little joke in the stately row of building façades along the canal. A famous Venetian-by-choice, the American Peggy Guggenheim, lived here. Mindful of her debt to the city, she succeeded in donating a truly fitting gift in the form of the museum which she put together to commemorate her great love for Venice.

When she bought this palazzo fragment in 1949, Europe was grey and impoverished by war, but that didn't affect Venice's beauty. Guggenheim liked the *Palazzo non compiuto*, the unfinished palace, because she could make her mark on it without having the monument authorities poking around. Europe's poverty didn't matter to this art-obsessed woman, who was born with several silver spoons in her mouth. In her heyday, she used to buy at least one picture per day, and she had a keen understanding of art not clouded by fashionable twaddle. Moreover, she made sure that her occasional temporary lovers like Max Ernst or Alexander Calder left her with a tangible proof of their genius.

Venice and modern art: the two generate constant tension. Everybody who visits the Biennale in the *Giardini* has seen how highly prized creations of extravagantly praised 'in' artists become totally invisible in the Venetian air and the light of the lagoons: Poof! they're gone! in spite of all the money and fuss they cost. The opposite happens in Peggy Guggenheim's Fragment Palace: simple objects, blue pieces of glass, for instance, little mobiles and gouaches suddenly take on an unsuspected radiance in the Lion Palace of the Venier family.

The Veniers started off with this palace in the middle of the eighteenth century. The waterfront side was decorated with eighteen lions, and it's said they kept live lions in the garden. This story about her house pleased Peggy Guggenheim, but it didn't intimidate her, for few people take such undisguised pleasure in wealth and the beautiful things money can do.

On the side facing the water, the admiring visitor is greeted by Mario Marini's figure of a rider, his arms spread out enthusiastically. To prove his uninhibited and confident joy and well-being, he extends his best part, prettily erect, toward male and female visitors and all the thousands of people who happen to pass by. The Prefect of Venice, who resided on the opposite bank of the Canal, was offended by this. Peggy (who certainly enjoyed other things besides money), felt that her *Angel of the Citadel*, as Marini called his work, looked most attractive in profile, and she would peek out of her salon windows during the afternoon to watch as people got worked up over the statue.

With its beautiful spaces and slight whiff of melancholy (the scent of loves long past), the Guggenheim is a stroke of luck, a place whose role as a museum will never get the upper hand or dominate the personal, the eccentrics, the flirts, or the farewells. The palace breathes, sheltering not only Peggy's spirit but also the spirits of the Venier family with their lions and the spirit of the Marquess Casati, who kept leopards instead of lions around 1910, and organized the so-called Diaghilev Parties, whatever those were. You can let your imagination run wild here. The Viscountess Castelrosso did that, keeping no known predators here but leaving behind six bathrooms and a splendid marble floor. She must also have invested lavishly in stucco and decorations, all of which Peggy had taken out again. Nothing is known about the viscountess's special parties, but later occupants – first the film mogul Douglas Fairbanks, Jr. and then the German, English and American armies of occupation – had their share.

Even before Peggy's takeover the palace was making friends with an overseas nonchalance. The garden, long empty of exotic beasts, is one of the largest and most beautiful in Venice, though you can't see it (or any of the other gardens, for that matter) from the outside. Ancient trees stand there, throwing their shadows on the works of Giacometti and Jean Arp, Brancusi, Calder, and Lipchitz. Peggy's collections are spread out in the house, too, where she has made laundry and servants' rooms, storage and guest rooms into gallery spaces, without sacrificing their private character.

Tancredi, whom she discovered, lived with and worked for her for a long time, while arguments and scenes reverberated throughout the house. Peggy wasn't unhappy when he finally moved out, because he had a tendency to get paint on his bare feet and then wander all around the palace.

Over time Peggy Guggenheim created a unique mixture of salon and gallery, museum and artists' meeting place. She dealt with occasional differences of opinion with great aplomb: 'When the nuns came to be blessed by the patriarch, who drove past my house in a motor boat on public holidays, I would take the phallus off the Rider sculpture and hide it in a drawer. (Note: With wise foresight, Marini had designed it to screw off!) I also did this on a number of occasions when I was receiving prudish visitors, but sometimes I forgot and was mortified at the sight of the phallus. In those cases there was nothing to do but ignore it. A legend started to go around Venice that I had several phalluses of different sizes – spare parts, you might say – which I used on different occasions.'

Gradually the great lover and unrelenting friend of art grew older. The big garden wasn't permanently deprived of animals, for the graves of Peggy's little dogs are lined up under a sign reading 'My beloved babies'. The life spans of the little dogs recorded there lead to the conclusion that she needed rather a long time to learn how to handle her babies. Not until the last years were her darlings granted an appropriate canine life span.

I saw Peggy Guggenheim still sitting in the garden where light fell diagonally through the trees, wearing comfortable slippers on her feet – a long, long way from her salad days. She had been expressing growing contempt for the art in Venice, and found the Biennale more pathetic every time she went – nothing but derivative trends from twenty years before, puffed up for the press. Some people took offence at her grouchiness because now that she belonged to the city, now that Venice had graciously deigned to accept her and her gift, everyone wanted her to sing the city's praises. She didn't go along with that. She held court modestly and somewhat grumpily, and her greatest joy was to look over at St. Mark's, knowing that her wonderful Pollocks were hanging behind it – in the only proper setting, at last. She hadn't had an easy time of it with Pollock; theirs was a hesitatingly begun but lasting love affair.

Sometimes if you go past the *Palazzo Guggenheim* at dusk, with red light falling on the happy Rider, you can look through the small door on the narrow side and see a figure sitting in a garden chair, bent forward with a small white dog at her feet.

Eva Demski, 'With Peggy Guggenheim'
from *Venedig – Salon der Welt. Achtzehn Stücke mit Begleitung* (1996)
(*Venice, the World's Salon. Eighteen essays with Accompaniment*)
translated by Susan Thorne

✳ ✳ ✳

The Venice Biennale was originally an art show held on alternate (odd) years, but now includes festivals of other art forms too, notably film. The art events are based in a park, the Giardini, where there are about thirty national pavilions along with a large hall for themed exhibitions. What were originally 'fringe' events at the Arsenale have become part of the official programme. A somewhat jaundiced view of the art on show at the Biennale is given by the protagonist of Geoff Dyer's Jeff in Venice, Death in Varanasi. *But don't let that put you off …*

It was too early to go to the Giardini – the perfect time to walk to the Accademia and see Giorgione's *Tempest* ahead of the crowds. Like everywhere else in Venice the museum was undergoing renovation but it was open – and there was no queue. A sign at the ticket desk announced SORRY WE HAVE NO AIR CONDITIONED. Another sign, smaller, in Italian, said something about Giorgione's *La Tempesta*. Bollocks … There was a simple rule of museum-going: if you had only one day free in a city, that would be the day the museum was closed. And if it *was* open, then the one piece you wanted to see would be out on loan or removed for restoration. But no, the sign simply explained that, due to renovation, *La Tempesta* had been moved, temporarily, to Room XIII. Jeff headed straight there.

No one else was around. He had the room and the painting to himself.

To one side of the picture a young mother is breast-feeding an infant, gazing out of the painting, meeting the eye of whoever is looking at it. Presumably she has just bathed in the river separating her from the elegantly dressed young man wedged into the bottom left-hand corner, leaning on a staff, gazing at her. He looks at her; she looks at us, looking at them. Whatever is going on, we are implicated in it. Behind them, in the background – though it isn't really background – a bridge spans the aquamarine river. Beyond the bridge a landscape-city crouches under the gathered clouds. A white bird, perhaps a stork, perches on the roof of one of the buildings. The sky is a wash of billowing, inky blue. A single line of white lightning crackles through the storm.

'The stoppage of time in Giorgione has a partly idyllic character. But the idyll is charged with presentiment,' McCarthy had written. 'Something frightening is about to happen.' This, Atman saw now, was slightly misleading. It was not only impossible to say what that 'something' was – let alone whether that something might be 'frightening' – it was impossible to tell whether it had happened in the past or would happen in the future, or would not happen at all. There was no before and no after, or at least they were indistinguishable from each other, interchangeable. Apart from that, what he saw now confirmed how precisely she had fixed the painting in words. It was, as she insisted, the stillness that produced the sense of unrest. [...]

Near the leafy entrance to the Giardini students and young artists handed out flyers for exhibitions of their own, alternative, semi-underground versions of the Biennale with music, DJs. The Giardini was already crowded by the time Jeff got inside, less than an hour after it had officially opened.

Patriotically, his first stop was the British pavilion, given over to Gilbert & George. In the 1980s, the critic Peter Fuller had conducted a vituperative crusade against Gilbert & George, seeing in them a threat to everything he held dear. By the time

Fuller was killed, in a car crash, he must have realized it had all been in vain, for Gilbert & George were poised to become godfathers to several generations of YBA hustlers – and now they had been honoured by having the British pavilion to themselves. The work, needless to say, was as weary as some harmless sin, the same old brightly-coloured, stained glass-looking nonsense they'd been doing for years, but the way Jeff looked at it (the only way one could look at it): who gave a shit? They were never going to do anything new, but so what? There was no point kicking against this affable pair of pricks.

From there he should have gone about things in a systematic fashion, ticking off each of the national pavilions in an orderly sequence, but there were already queues of art immigrants waiting to get into Canada and France – whose pavilions were next to Britain's – so he skipped them and started dropping into places in a completely haphazard fashion. From G & G he went to the Norwegian pavilion, which featured a wall of yellow and black Op Art circles. Except they weren't circles, they were targets, dartboards, an entire wall of them. Some distance away there were large cardboard boxes of green and red darts, which you could aim at the wall, gradually altering the overall pattern and distribution of colour. Jeff had just aimed the last of a handful of red darts when someone called his name and threw a dart in his eyes. […]

Along with the national pavilions at the Giardini, the Arsenale was the other key component of the Biennale: a selection of work by artists from around the world, chosen or commissioned by the director of the Biennale and united (allegedly) by some kind of theme. That this theme was impossible to discern from the apparently random array of art on display did not diminish the experience – or not Jeff's experience, at any rate. There was a ton of stuff to see: paintings, installations, photographs, video streams, sculpture (sort of), even, quaintly, the odd drawing.

Geoff Dyer, *Jeff in Venice, Death in Varanasi* (2009)

✳ ✳ ✳

*And if you're not an art enthusiast, Venice has plenty
of other cultural entertainment to offer in the form of
theatre, opera, and music. Carlo Goldoni (1707–93),
the city's most famous playwright, held a mirror up to
the local population.*

The first public opera house, at Saint Cassiano, opened for the
Carnival season of 1637, and by 1700, there were ten opera
houses in Venice with a repertory of more than 350 operas.
And what if instead of opera being sacred or classical, we made
it funny? Baldassare Galuppi came up with opera buffa.

Improv comedy was another natural fit, although the
commedia dell'arte, with its classical roots, had spread through
Italy from Naples. Venice had dozens of private, public, clois-
tered, and open-to-the-street theatres in the eighteenth century.
In its early manifestation, the dominant form throughout Italy
was what we would now call scripted improv, with sketched
plots on which stock characters – foolish lovers, pompous
braggarts, insolent servants, domineering wives, sharp swin-
dlers, saucy gold-diggers – improvised. When this began to
grow predictable and tiresome, the thought occurred to Carlo
Goldoni: "I can do better than that. What if I updated the characters and wrote their lines for them?"

One might say that reality theatre was a Venetian invention.

Judith Martin, *No Vulgar Hotel* (2007)

✳ ✳ ✳

*A vivid and entertaining account of his theatrical
experiences in Venice is given by Johann Wolfgang
von Goethe.*

3 October (1786)

Last night I went to the opera in San Mosè (here the theatres are
named after the nearest church) and did not enjoy it much. The

libretto, the music and the singers lacked that essential energy which such performances need to reach perfection. One could not say that everything was bad, but only the two women took the trouble to act well and to please. That, at least, was something to be thankful for. Both had beautiful figures and good voices and were lively, agreeable little creatures. The men, on the other hand, sang without any gusto and their voices lacked all brilliance.

The ballet was deficient in ideas and was booed most of the time. But one or two of the dancers, male and female, were wildly applauded. The girls considered it their duty to acquaint the audience with every beautiful part of their bodies.

4 October

At the Teatro San Luca yesterday I saw an improvised comedy, played in masks with great bravura. The actors were, of course, unequal. Pantalone, very good; one woman, without being an outstanding actress, had an excellent delivery and stage presence. The subject was a fantastic one, similar to that which is played in our country under the title *Der Verschlag*.

We were entertained for more than three hours with one incredible situation after the other. But once again, the basis of everything is the common people; the spectators join in the play and the crowd becomes part of the theatre. During the daytime, squares, canals, gondolas and palazzi are full of life as the buyer and the seller, the beggar and the boatman, the housewife and the lawyer offer something for sale, sing and gamble, shout and swear. In the evening these same people go to the theatre to behold their actual life, presented with greater economy as make-believe interwoven with fairy stories and removed from reality by masks, yet, in its characters and manners, the life they know. They are delighted, like children, shouting, clapping and generally making a din. From sunset to sunset, from midnight to midnight, they are just the same. Indeed, I never saw more natural acting than that of these masked players, an art which can only be achieved by an extraordinarily happy nature and long practice.

5 October At night

I have just got back from the Tragedy and am still laughing, so let me commit this farce to paper at once. The piece was not bad; the author had jumbled together all the tragic matadors, and the actors had good roles. Most of the situations were stale, but a few were fresh and quite felicitous. Two fathers who hated each other, the sons and daughters of these divided families passionately in love crosswise, one couple even secretly married. Violent, cruel things went on and in the end nothing remained to make the young people happy but that their fathers should stab one another, whereupon the curtain fell to thundering applause. The audience did not stop shouting '*fuora*' until the two leading couples condescended to creep round from behind one side of the curtain, make their bows and go off on the other.

The audience was still not satisfied but continued clapping and shouting '*I morti!*' until the two dead men also appeared and bowed, whereupon a few voices cried: '*Bravi I morti*'; and it was some time before they were allowed to make their exit. To get the full flavour of this absurdity, one must see and hear it for oneself. My ears are ringing with the *bravo! bravi!* Which Italians are for ever shouting, and now I have even heard the dead acclaimed with this compliment.

10 October

At last I have seen a real comedy! At the Teatro San Luca today they played *La Baruffe Chiozzotte*, one of the few plays by Goldoni which is still performed. The title might be roughly translated as *The Scuffles and Brawls in Chioggia*. The characters are all natives of that town, fishermen and their wives, sisters and daughters. The habitual to-do made by these people, their quarrels, their outbursts of temper, their good nature, superficiality, wit, humour and natural behaviour – all these were excellently imitated. [...]

I have never in my life witnessed such an ecstasy of joy as that shown by the audience when they saw themselves and their families so realistically portrayed on the stage. They shouted with laughter and approval from beginning to end. The actors did an excellent job. Between them they represented all the types of character one finds among the common people. The leading lady was particularly charming – much better than she was the other day as a tragic heroine. By and large, all the actresses, but especially this one, imitated the voices, gestures and temperaments of the people with uncanny skill, but the highest praise is due to the playwright for creating such a delightful entertainment out of thin air. Only someone in intimate contact with this pleasure-loving people could have done it. It is written with an expert hand.

Johann Wolfgang von Goethe, *Italian Journey* (1786–1788)
translated by W. H. Auden and Elizabeth Mayer

❋ ❋ ❋

*Another eighteenth-century writer, English essayist
Joseph Addison, recalls the various theatrical entertainments then on offer in Venice, as well as the 'street
theatre' of Carnival time.*

The carnival of Venice is everywhere talked of. The great diversion of the place at that time, as well as on all other high occasions, is masking. The Venetians, who are naturally grave, love to give in to the follies and entertainments of such seasons, when disguised in a false personage. [...] These disguises give occasion to abundance of love-adventures; for there is something more intriguing in the amours of Venice than in those of other countries, and I question not but the secret history of a carnival would make a collection of very diverting novels.

Operas are another great entertainment of this season. The poetry of them is generally as exquisitely ill, as the music is good. The arguments are often taken from some celebrated action of the ancient Greeks or Romans, which sometimes looks ridiculous enough; for who can endure to hear one of the rough old Romans squeaking through the mouth of an eunuch, especially when they may choose a subject out of courts where eunuchs are really actors, or represent them by any of the soft Asiatic monarchs? [...]

The comedies that I saw at Venice, or indeed in any other part of Italy, are very different, and more lewd than those of other countries. Their poets have no notion of genteel comedy, and fall into the most filthy double-meanings imaginable, when they have a mind to make their audience merry.

Joseph Addison, *Essays* (c.1703)

✵ ✵ ✵

And then there's the theatre on the water ...

Processionals put theatre in the streets and regattas put theatre on the canals. The very word regatta is of ancient Venetian coinage, only coming into English in 1652 in a description of a Venetian event. Doges and procurators fairly leapt with eagerness to add a regatta and ducal procession to every noteworthy occurrence, whether political, religious, or social. The king of France or the Hapsburg emperor is coming to visit, let's have a regatta; an important dynastic marriage is arranged between merchant families – pull out those skiffs and multicolour jerkins, we're having a regatta. A plot uncovered, a plague ended, a treaty signed, start tarring those hulls, it's regatta time. Eventually, Venetian rowing clubs were organising regattas without the pretext of a holiday. By the eighteenth century, important events needn't even be connected to a regatta; competitions between rowing clubs themselves became sufficient impetus, and not just for men. From the late fifteenth century, women's crews had a place on the canal as well. Regattas could be professional or processional, cortège or competition.

Judith Martin, *No Vulgar Hotel* (2007)

✳ ✳ ✳

Music in the city is inevitably associated with Venetian-born composer Antonio Vivaldi (1678–1741). But this can have its drawbacks. Judith Martin again ...

Venice does abound in musical offerings. It was always a centre of music, with little opera houses everywhere and composers on frantic deadlines churning out pieces still beloved by audiences today. In a brilliant pairing of supply with demand, Venice provided its orphans, of which the romantic city had more than its share, with music lessons. Vivaldi, the Red Priest (for his hair, not his politics), trained such successful All-Girl Orchestras at the church of the Pietà that a warning to rich and ambitious parents not to abandon their daughters at the Pietà for free music lessons is chiselled into the side of the building.

Vivaldi's posthumous reputation was in eclipse in the twentieth century until he was rescued by a Venetophile. Olga Rudge, the violinist and musicologist who lived in Venice with Ezra Pound, is credited with starting the Vivaldi revival in the 1930s, turning up and publishing lost works, giving Vivaldi concerts, and founding the Venetian Vivaldi Society. We have long since ceased to thank her. As we explain to newcomers, the good news is that there is a choice of small concerts in Venice every night. The bad news is that they all play Vivaldi.

'But I like Vivaldi,' newcomers are wont to declare. When they've been treated to him for four or five concerts in a row, and have been several times importuned on the street by teenagers in ill-pressed eighteenth-century costumes to come to a concert at 'Vivaldi's church' (he was dead when the present one was rebuilt on the site) by touring high school orchestras, they reconsider. So we check the posters and listings, and offer a prize to anyone who can find a concert that doesn't feature Vivaldi or, failing that, one that at least isn't playing the *Four Seasons*.

Judith Martin, *No Vulgar Hotel* (2007)

* * *

The famed 'musicality' of Venetians no doubt goes back to ancient traditions of the boatmen's singing, described here by Goethe.

7 October (1786)

For this evening I had made arrangements to hear the famous singing of the boatmen, who chant verses by Tasso and Ariosto to their own melodies. This performance has to be ordered in advance, for it is now rarely done and belongs, rather, to the half-forgotten legends of the past. The moon had risen when I took my seat in a gondola and the two singers, one in the prow, the other in the stern, began chanting verse after verse in turns. The melody, which we know from Rousseau, is something between chorale and recitative. It always moves at the same tempo without any definite beat. The modulation is of the same character; the singers change pitch according to the content of the verse in a kind of declamation.

I shall not go into the question of how the melody evolved. It is enough to say that it is ideal for someone idly singing to himself and adapting the tune to poems he knows by heart.

The singer sits on the shore of the island, on the bank of a canal or in a gondola, and sings at the top of his voice – the people here appreciate volume more than anything else. His aim is to make his voice carry as far as possible over the still mirror of the water. Far away another singer hears it. He knows the melody and the words and answers with the next verse. The first singer answers again and so on. Each is the echo of the other. They keep this up night after night without ever getting tired. If the listener has chosen the right spot, which is halfway between them, the further apart they are, the more enchanting the singing will sound.

To demonstrate this, my boatmen tied up the gondola on the shore of the Giudecca and walked along the canal in opposite directions. I walked back and forth, leaving the one, who was just about to sing, and walking towards the other, who had just stopped.

For the first time I felt the full effect of this singing. The sound of their voices far away was extraordinary, a lament without sadness, and I was moved to tears. I put this down to my mood at the moment, but my old manservant said: '*è singolare, come quel canto intenerisce, e molto più, quando è più ben cantato.*' He wanted me to hear the women on the Lido, especially those from Malamocco and Pellestrina. They, too, he told me, sang verses by Tasso to the same or a similar melody, and added: 'It is their custom to sit on the seashore while their husbands are out sea-fishing, and sing these songs in penetrating tones until, from far out over the sea, their men reply, and in this way they converse with each other.' Is this not a beautiful custom? I dare say that, to someone standing close by, the sound of such voices, competing with the thunder of the waves, might not be very agreeable. But the motive behind such singing is so human and genuine that it makes the mere notes of the melody, over which scholars have racked their brains in vain, come to life. It is the cry of some lonely human being sent out into the wide world till it reaches the ears of another lonely human being who is moved to answer it.

Johann Wolfgang von Goethe, *Italian Journey* (1786–1788)
translated by W. H. Auden and Elizabeth Mayer

✳ ✳ ✳

Venice is famed for its opera. La Fenice, which has been called the world's most beautiful opera house,

*saw the premières of many great operas. John Berendt
provides a vivid account of the January evening when
it burned down.*

It happened on Monday evening, 29 January 1996.

Shortly before nine o'clock, Archimede Seguso sat down at
the dinner table and unfolded his napkin. Before joining him,
his wife went into the living room to lower the curtains, which
was her long-standing evening ritual. [...]

Signora Seguso paused to look out of the window before
lowering the curtain. She noticed that the air had become hazy,
and she mused aloud that a winter fog had set in. In response,
Signor Seguso remarked from the other room that it must have
come in very quickly, because he had seen the quarter moon in
a clear sky only a few minutes before.

The living-room window looked across a small canal at the
back of the Fenice Opera House, thirty feet away. Rising above
it in the distance, some hundred yards away, the theatre's grand
entrance wing appeared to be shrouded in mist. Just as she
started to lower the curtain, Signora Seguso saw a flash. She
thought it was lightning. Then she saw another flash, and this
time she knew it was fire.

'Papa!' she cried out. 'The Fenice is on fire!'

Signor Seguso came quickly to the window. More flames
flickered at the front of the theatre, illuminating what Signora
Seguso had thought was mist but had in fact been smoke. She
rushed to the telephone and dialled 115 for the fire brigade.
Signor Seguso went into his bedroom and stood at the corner
window, which was even closer to the Fenice than the living-
room window.

Between the fire and the Segusos' house lay a jumble of buildings that constituted the Fenice. The part on fire was farthest
away, the chaste neoclassical entrance wing with its formal
reception rooms, known collectively as the Apollonian rooms.
Then came the main body of the theatre with its elaborately

rococo auditorium, and finally the vast backstage area. Flaring out from both sides of the auditorium and the backstage were clusters of smaller, interconnected buildings like the one that housed the scenery workshop immediately across the narrow canal from Signor Seguso.

The enormity of what was happening outside his window stunned Signor Seguso. The Gran Teatro La Fenice was one of the splendours of Venice; it was arguably the most beautiful opera house in the world, and one of the most significant. The Fenice had commissioned dozens of operas that had premiered on its stage – Verdi's *La Traviata* and *Rigoletto*, Igor Stravinsky's *The Rake's Progress*, Benjamin Britten's *The Turn of the Screw*. For two hundred years, audiences had delighted in the sumptuous clarity of the Fenice's acoustics, the magnificence of its five tiers of gilt-encrusted boxes, and the baroque fantasy of it all. […]

Signor Seguso stood silently at his bedroom window, watching as the flames raced across the entire top floor of the entrance wing. He knew that, for all its storeyed loveliness, the Fenice was at this moment an enormous pile of exquisite kindling. Inside a thick shell of Istrian stone lined with brick, the structure was made entirely of wood – wooden beams, wooden floors, wooden walls – richly embellished with wood carvings, sculpted stucco, and papier-mâché, all of it covered with layer upon layer of lacquer and gilt. Signor Seguso was aware, too, that the scenery workshop just across the canal from his house was stocked with solvents and, most worrying of all, cylinders of propane gas that were used for welding and soldering.

Signora Seguso came back into the room to say that she had finally spoken to the police.

'They already knew about the fire,' she said. 'They told me we should leave the house at once.' […]

The Segusos' house was only one of many buildings close to the Fenice. Except for Campo San Fantin, a small plaza at the front of the theatre, the Fenice was hemmed in by old and equally flammable buildings, many of them attached to it or separated from it by only four or five feet. This was not at all unusual in Venice, where building space had always been at a premium. Seen from above, Venice resembled a jigsaw puzzle of terracotta rooftops. Passages between some of the buildings were so narrow one could not walk through them with an open umbrella. It had become a speciality of Venetian burglars to escape from the scene of a crime by leaping from roof to roof. If the fire in the Fenice were able to make the same sort of leap, it would almost certainly destroy a sizeable swath of Venice. [...]

The Fenice was now ringed by a tumult of shouts and running footsteps. Tenants, routed from their houses by the police, crossed paths with patrons coming out of the Ristorante Antico Martini. A dozen bewildered guests rolled suitcases out of the Hotel La Fenice, asking directions to the Hotel Saturnia, where they had been told to go. Into their midst, a wild-eyed woman wearing only a nightgown came stumbling from her house into Campo San Fantin screaming hysterically. She threw herself to the ground in front of the theatre, flailing her arms and rolling on the pavement. Several waiters came out of the Antico Martini and led her inside.

Two fireboats managed to navigate to a water-filled canal a short distance from the Fenice. The hoses were not long enough to reach round the intervening buildings, however, so the firemen dragged them through the kitchen window at the back of the Antico Martini and out through the dining room into Campo San Fantin. They aimed their nozzles at flames burning furiously in a top-floor window of the theatre, but the water pressure was too low. The arc of water barely reached the windowsill. The fire went on leaping and taunting and sucking up great turbulent currents of air that set the flames flapping like brilliant red sails in a violent wind.

Several policemen struggled with the massive front door of the Fenice, but to no avail. One of them drew his pistol and fired three shots at the lock. The door opened. Two firemen rushed in and disappeared into a dense white wall of smoke. Moments later they came running out. 'It's too late,' said one. 'It's burning like straw.'

The wail of sirens now filled the air as police and firemen raced up and down the Grand Canal in motorboats, spanking up huge butterfly wings of spray as they bounced through the wakes of other boats. About an hour after the first alarm, the city's big fire launch pulled up at the landing stage behind Haig's Bar. Its high-powered rigs would at last be able to pump water the two hundred yards from the Grand Canal to the Fenice. Dozens of firemen ran hoses from the fire launch into Campo Santa Maria del Giglio, feverishly coupling sections together, but it was immediately apparent that the hoses were of different gauges. Leaks sprayed from the couplings, but the firemen carried the linked hoses, such as they were, up to the rooftops around the Fenice anyway. They directed half of the water on to the theatre and the rest of it on to adjacent buildings. Fire Commandant Alfio Pini had already made a momentous strategic decision: the Fenice was lost; save the city.

John Berendt, *City of Falling Angels* (2005)

✳ ✳ ✳

Venice often finds itself the location for sinister doings in both literature and films. Judith Martin has something to say on the subject.

A possible source of Venice's high water that has not been investigated is the Archimedes' Principle Problem: the number of dead bodies that filmmakers and mystery writers have been slipping into cold canals under cover of night.

Using Venice as a crime scene, a notoriously impractical idea to criminals, is an irresistible one to crime fans. Murder mysteries and sinister cinema have surpassed even the Napoleonic regime in picturing Venice as a legal and moral disaster area. To Napoleon's success in convincing the world of the evils of a government that was (unlike his own) staffed by rotating public servants with strictly limited terms and checks and balances, they have added the evils of a menacing citizenry skilled in sadism. The result is that Venice's considerable presence in literature and drama is as unpoliced police state, as it were, where officials vie with the population in committing and concealing atrocities.

The natural result ought to be that honest folk from elsewhere would be anxious to escape its contaminated clutches. As we know, that is hardly the case. It could be the attraction, of course. Still, word must have gotten around by now that Venice is disappointingly safe.

Judith Martin, *No Vulgar Hotel* (2007)

✻ ✻ ✻

One of the best known stories to use Venice as a sinister mise en scène is Daphne du Maurier's Don't Look Now, made into a spine-chilling film, in 1973, starring Julie Christie and Donald Sutherland. Here's a taster.

They went out laughing into the warm soft night, and the magic was about them everywhere. 'Let's walk,' he said, 'let's walk and work up an appetite for our gigantic meal,' and inevitably they found themselves by the Molo and the lapping gondolas dancing upon the water, the lights everywhere blending with the darkness. There were other couples strolling for the same sake of aimless enjoyment, backwards, forwards, purposeless, and the inevitable sailors in groups, noisy, gesticulating, and dark-eyed girls whispering, clicking on high heels.

'The trouble is,' said Laura, 'walking in Venice becomes compulsive once you start. Just over the next bridge, you say, and then the next one beckons. I'm sure there are no restaurants down here, we're almost at those public gardens where they hold the Biennale. Let's turn back. I know there's a restaurant somewhere near the church of San Zaccaria, there's a little alley-way leading to it.'

'Tell you what,' said John, 'if we go down here by the Arsenal, and cross that bridge at the end and head left, we'll come upon San Zaccaria from the other side. We did it the other morning.'

'Yes, but it was daylight then. We may lose our way, it's not very well lit.'

'Don't fuss. I have an instinct for these things.'

They turned down the Fondamenta dell'Arsenale and crossed the little bridge short of the Arsenal itself, and so on past the church of San Martino. There were two canals ahead, one bearing right, the other left, with narrow streets beside them. John hesitated. Which one was it they had walked beside the day before?

'You see,' protested Laura, 'we shall be lost, just as I said.'

'Nonsense,' replied John firmly. 'It's the left-hand one, I remember the little bridge.'

The canal was narrow, the houses on either side seemed to close in upon it, and in the daytime, with the sun's reflection on the water and the windows of the houses open, bedding upon the balconies, a canary singing in a cage, there had been an impression of warmth, of secluded shelter. Now, ill-lit, almost in darkness, the windows of the houses shuttered, the water dank, the scene appeared altogether different, neglected, poor, and the long narrow boats moored to the slippery steps of cellar entrances looked like coffins.

'I swear I don't remember this bridge,' said Laura, pausing, and holding on to the rail, 'and I don't like the look of that alley-way beyond.'

'There's a lamp halfway up,' John told her. 'I know exactly where we are, not far from the Greek quarter.'

They crossed the bridge, and were about to plunge into the alley-way when they heard the cry. It came, surely, from one of the houses on the opposite side, but which one it was impossible to say. With the shutters closed each one of them seemed dead. They turned, and stared in the direction from which the sound had come.

'What was it?' whispered Laura.

'Some drunk or other,' said John briefly. 'Come on.'

Less like a drunk than someone being strangled, and the choking cry suppressed as the grip held firm.

'We ought to call the police,' said Laura.

'Oh, for heaven's sake,' said John. Where did she think she was – Piccadilly?

'Well, I'm off, it's sinister,' she replied, and began to hurry away up the twisting alley-way. John hesitated, his eye caught by a small figure which suddenly crept from a cellar entrance below one of the opposite houses, and then jumped into a narrow boat below. It was a child, a little girl – she couldn't have been more than five or six – wearing a short coat over her minute skirt, a pixie hood covering her head. There were four boats moored, line upon line, and she proceeded to jump from one to the other with surprising agility, intent, it would seem, upon escape. Once her foot slipped and he caught his breath, for she was within a few feet of the water, losing balance; then she recovered, and hopped on to the furthest boat. Bending, she tugged at the rope, which had the effect of swinging the boat's after-end across the canal, almost touching the opposite side and another cellar entrance, about thirty feet from the spot where John stood watching her. Then the child jumped again, landing upon the cellar steps, and vanished into the house, the boat swinging back into mid-canal behind her. The whole episode could not have taken more than four minutes. Then he heard the quick patter of feet. Laura had returned. She had seen none of it, for which he felt unspeakably thankful. The sight of a child, a little girl, in what must have been near danger, her fear that the scene he had just witnessed was in some way a

194

sequel to the alarming cry, might have had a disastrous effect on her overwrought nerves.

'What are you doing?' she called. 'I daren't go on without you. The wretched alley branches in two directions.'

'Sorry,' he told her. 'I'm coming.'

He took her arm and they walked briskly along the alley, John with an apparent confidence he did not posses.

'There were no more cries, were there?' she asked.

'No,' he said, 'no, nothing. I tell you, it was some drunk.'

The alley led to a deserted *campo* behind a church, not a church he knew, and he led the way across, along another street and over a further bridge.

'Wait a minute,' he said. 'I think we take this right-hand turning. It will lead us into the Greek quarter – the church of San Georgio is somewhere over there.'

She did not answer. She was beginning to lose faith. The place was like a maze. They might circle round and round forever, and then find themselves back again, near the bridge where they had heard the cry. Doggedly he led her on, and then surprisingly, with relief, he saw people walking in the lighted street ahead, there was a spire of a church, the surroundings became familiar.

'There, I told you,' he said. 'That's San Zaccaria, we've found it all right. Your restaurant can't be far away.'

And anyway, there would be other restaurants, somewhere to eat, at least here was the cheering glitter of lights, of movement, canals beside which people walked, the atmosphere of tourism. The letters 'Ristorante', in blue lights, shone like a beacon down a left-hand alley.

'Is this your place?' he asked.

'God knows,' she said. 'Who cares? Let's feed there anyway.'

And so into the sudden blast of heated air and hum of voices, the smell of pasta, wine, waiters, jostling customers, laughter. 'For two? This way, please.' Why, he thought, was one's British nationality always so obvious? A cramped little table and an enormous menu scribbled in an indecipherable mauve biro, with the waiter hovering, expecting the order forthwith.

'Two very large camparis, with soda,' John said. '*Then* we'll study the menu.'

Daphne du Maurier, *Don't Look Now* (1971)

❊ ❊ ❊

Susan Hill uses the potentially chaotic atmosphere of Carnival time for her haunting mystery The Man in the Picture.

The first hour or two of the festival was tremendous fun. The streets were full of people on their way to join the procession, the shops had some sort of special cakes baking and the smell filled the night air. There were drummers and dancers and people playing pipes on every corner, and many of the balconies had flags and garlands hanging from them. I am trying to remember how it felt, to be lighthearted, to be full of happiness, walking through the city with Anne, such a short time ago.

St. Mark's Square was thronged and there was music coming from every side. We walked along the Riva degli Schiavoni and back, moving slowly with the long procession, and as we returned, the fireworks began over the water, lighting the sky and the ancient buildings and the canal itself in greens and blues, reds and golds in turn. Showers of crystals and silver and gold dust shot up into the air, the rockets soared. It was spectacular. I was so happy to be part of it.

We walked along the canal, in and out of the alleys and squares, until we came down between high buildings again to a spot facing the bridge.

The jetty was thronged with people. All of those who had been processing must have been there and we were pushed and jostled by people trying to get to the front beside the canal, where the gondolas were lined up waiting to take people to the festivities on the opposite bank. The fireworks were still exploding in all directions so that every few minutes there was a collective cry or sigh of wonder from the crowd. And then I noticed that some of them were wearing the costumes of the carnival: the ancient Venetian figures of the Old Woman, the Fortune Teller, the Doctor, the Barber, the Man with the Monkey, Pulcinello, and Death with his scythe mingled among us, their faces concealed by low hats and masks and paint, eyes gleaming here and there. I was suddenly stricken with panic. I had not meant to be here. I wanted to leave, urgently, to go back to our quiet square and sit at the café over a drink in the balmy evening. I turned to Anne.

But she was not at my side. Somehow, she had been hidden from me by the ever-changing crowd. I pushed my way between bodies urgently, calling her name. I turned to see if she was behind me. And as I turned, the blood stopped in my veins. My heart itself seemed to cease beating. My mouth was dry and my tongue felt swollen and I could not speak Anne's name.

I glimpsed, a yard or two away, a figure wearing a white silk mask studded with sequins and with a white plume of feathers in her dark hair. I caught her eyes, dark and huge and full of hatred.

I struggled to my left, towards the alleyway, away from the water, away from the gondolas rocking and swaying, away from the masks and the figures and the brilliant lights of the fireworks that kept exploding and cascading down again towards the dark water. I lost sight of the woman and when I looked back again she had gone.

I ran then, ran and ran, calling out to Anne, shouting for help, screaming in the end as I searched frantically through all the twists and turns of Venice for my wife.

I came back to the hotel. I alerted the police. I was forced to wait to give them Anne's description. They said that visitors to Venice get lost every day, …

Susan Hill, *The Man in the Picture* (2007)

✳ ✳ ✳

Despite the sinister spin sometimes put upon Venice's
Carnival in literature and films, it is the entertain-
ment for which the city is probably most famous. The
word 'Carnival' – or Carnevale, in Italian – comes
from 'saying farewell' ('vale') to meat ('carne'), for
the period of Lent, six weeks before Easter. But it's
really just an excuse for one big communal party.

The colourful celebration swirling through the streets was actually a recent revival of the centuries-old Venetian festival. Napoleon had put an end to it when he defeated the Venetian Republic.
By then Carnival had reached the height of decadence, having
grown from a two-week period of merry-making to six months
of parties, dances, spectacles, games, and walking around Venice
behind masks, incognito. It was not until the late 1970s that a
serious revival took place; it was prompted in part by Federico
Fellini's exotic and surreal 1976 film *Casanova*. The reincarna-
tion of Carnival started in a small way, on the island of Burano
and in working-class districts, with plays and costume parties
in the local squares. Before long the revels became citywide,
then tourists started joining in, and finally an industry grew up
around them, the most noticeable feature being the mask shops
opening all over Venice. They were little nooks of colour and
fantasy, their stage-lit windows lighting up darkened side-streets
all year long. Soon masks were a favourite tourist icon. But with
the appearance of each new mask shop, there always seemed to
be one fewer greengrocer, one fewer bakery, one fewer butcher's
shop, to the consternation of Venetians, who found themselves
having to walk twice as far to buy a tomato or a loaf of bread.
Mask shops became a detested symbol of the city's capitulation
to tourism at the expense of its liveability.

One mask shop, however, was spared any such opprobrium.
It was Mondonovo, the studio of Guerrino Lovato, a sculptor

and set designer, who had been instrumental in resurrecting Carnival back in the days when it was attended only by Venetians. Lovato had started making masks in his sculpture studio, almost as a public service. They were a beloved novelty, and his studio became the first mask shop in Venice. [...]

Carnival had begun. Narrow streets that had been easily passable for the last few weeks were now solid with tourists, shuffling along in masks and fanciful hats with bells. Venetians no longer had Venice all to themselves, but at least there was the saving grace of a buoyant, lighthearted spirit. The partygoing masquerade rolled through every quarter of the city. It spilled into shops, museums, and restaurants, and floated along the canals on gondolas, water taxis, and *vaporetti*. Even the taste buds rejoiced with the reappearance of the Carnival pastry, *frittelle* – small, sweet fritters studded with raisins and pine nuts and, if one chose, filled with zabaglione or vanilla cream.

Into this madhouse vision of eighteenth-century Venice slipped an unassuming figure who was joined by Mayor Cacciari and a mob of reporters and photographers. Woody Allen had come to Venice to pay his respects to the city he loved and where his jazz band were to have given a concert two weeks hence to reopen a renovated Fenice Opera House. Instead, he said, he would now give a concert at the Goldoni Theatre as a benefit for the Fenice.

John Berendt, *City of Falling Angels* (2005)

❊ ❊ ❊

A few more facts about Carnival, from Juan Manuel de Prada.

The carnival had reached illustrious heights during the most dire and fateful periods in the Republic's history, when epidemics of the plague were at their worst, and the air was poisoned by the deadly vapours given off by the corpses piled up on one or other of the islands, or on neighbourhood dunghills. Healthy members of society, and those still able to mask their bubonic tumours with rice powder, contracted the disease in the orgiastic frenzy that was a euphoric reflection of the other contagion that was due to carry them off. Carnivals lasted for months, until Lent, and to the buboes caused by the plague were added those of syphilis, passed from one to another in the promiscuous behaviour made easy by masked anonymity. In order not to introduce a note of discord into the festive copulating of the multitude, the doctors and surgeons who were responsible for public health at the time dreamed up for their own use a distinctive type of breathing apparatus inside a mask that had a hollow beak filled with disinfectant substances which they inhaled, to protect themselves from the fetid air around. This mask, which, at first, was regarded as intimidating and ill-omened – the Venetians fled from those who wore it in the way we avoid those dismal great birds that feed on carrion – ended up by becoming an acceptable feature of carnival, and took its place in the list of its characters, most of which were derived from the *commedia dell'arte*: Harlequin, Columbine, Pulcinello, and the rest of them.

Juan Manuel de Prada, *The Tempest* (1997)
translated by Paul Antill

❋ ❋ ❋

In Libby Purves's novel More Lives Than One, *a courageous and dedicated school teacher takes a group of children to Venice at Carnival time to widen their limited horizons while giving them fun and an experience they will never forget.*

Three hours later, in wild exhilaration at the sights they had seen, sore feet and sleepiness forgotten, the children tore back into the quiet *pensione* and, with difficulty, piled into Kit's tiny room. He heaved his big brown suitcase onto the bed, pushing children aside to make space for it, and opened the lid.

There, neatly folded as Nellie Armstrong had put them away after a ragged summer production of *Dracula, The Musical*, were piles of long full cloaks of thin black cotton. The sides were gathered into rough sleeves, so that when the wearer raised an arm, the scalloped form of a bat's wing appeared beneath it. On top of these, thicker and shinier, were stiff black linen masks made like bags with eyeholes and pointed ears. The contents of the suitcase were sufficient to costume a chorus of sixteen vampire bats.

Kit pulled out a larger hat and put it on his own head. His eyes gleamed through the holes and he raised his arms, still in his floppy black coat, into a reasonable semblance of a giant bat. With trills of glee, the children grabbed for the cloaks, boys and girls equally excited, weariness forgotten in the exhilaration of setting out into this weird and beautiful city in disguise.

'We could make *bat noises*!'

'Yeah, did you see those people by the big tower, that was all penguins?'

'Did you see the big bird, with the fevers?'

'Did you see the huge big hat with the red things and the wire?'

'An' the cat lady?'

'There was hundreds of cat ladies, stupid.'

'The one with the big silver whiskers!'

Kit smiled inside his bat hat. The jolt had happened. On the far side of it, teaching could begin. They were no longer lumpen children of a lumpen land, resistant to anything new or strange or difficult, liable to whine at missing *Eastenders* (as Natalie and Leanne had done the previous night at the Gare de Lyon). They were all his now, ready for anything. Liberated by the strange, stagey city in carnival they would soak up anything offered to them.

They had already learned that a seventeenth-century diarist could be right. Now he could read them anything at all about

Venice – Ruskin, Byron, Henry James, Wordsworth, Thomas Mann – and young as they were they would listen, and at least want to understand. He could take them away from the carnival crowds to show them melancholy corners: the brooding quiet of San Michele, the horses of St Mark in their high eminence, the hypnotic swirling and waving patterns of a hundred mosaic pavements, the glassworks of Murano. They would see now with clear eyes and heightened emotions, grope for language to express what they saw, and understand in doing so the power that language holds. They would gain memories, have their dreams fed and thoughts freed by glittering excess and ancient beauty. Morrey Hart had stood half an hour ago in the centre of St Mark's Square, spread his arms wide and said, 'It's like being on a rollercoaster, only not moving.'

As Kit contemplated his troop of small bats a wave of love swept over him, almost choking him.

Libby Purves, *More Lives Than One* (1998)

* * *

In Venice, even a political demonstration can take the form of carnival-style street theatre. Here's a recent example.

For some time, the people behind the passionately pro-Venice website Venessia.com, have promised that they would do something to show their pain if the city's population dropped below 60,000. The exodus of real Venetians is recorded weekly in an illuminated display – the Venetian-counter – in the window of the Morelli pharmacy at Rialto. This month, for the first time, we are down to 59, 984. The streets of Venice each day now hold fewer Venetians than tourists.

Venessia.com maintains that Venice has not died a natural death but been assassinated by mismanagement, greed and stupidity. It comes down to housing. If the city does not provide houses for young couples, how can young couples provide new Venetians for the city?

In response to the sinking numbers, Venessia.com decided to do what Venice has always done *in extremis*: throw a masked party, in which the macabre would mix with the ironic, the burlesque with the profound. A furious discussion breaks out in the city. People start sending 'telegrams of condolence' for the dead city to Venessia.com.

November 14th dawns moody grey and morbidly humid. Grim-faced locals and stupefied tourists swarm at Rialto. The deceased city, represented by a hot-pink coffin draped with the Venetian flag, is being floated up the canal on a *balotina,* in which stands the black-cloaked actor Cesare Colonnese, his face made up in a deathly pallor. Even so, it cannot express quite enough tragedy: he carries another mask of pain mounted on a stick. The *balotina* follows a barge in which a grand piano is played by Paolo Zanarella, his black cloak flowing behind him.

At 11.55 the riot police arrive and arrange themselves under the portico of the town hall. (City officials, who have scoffed at the idea of the funeral, are nowhere to be seen). At 11.55 the international press disembarks from crowded taxis, for Venessia.com has caught not just the city's but the world's imagination with its gesture. At 12.00 the funeral procession arrives at Rialto, escorted by police boats. As they pass under the bridge, the rowers raise their oars in solemn salute to the crowd. The coffin is lifted on the shoulders of the chief mourners and carried along the *passarelle* into the portico, accompanied by a funeral bouquet in the Venetian colours of yellow and maroon. There's another huge bouquet made of slivers of paper – the telegrams of condolence. Gilberto Gasparini reads out a long poem of lament and betrayal. Cesare Colonnese pronounces the funeral oration in Venetian.

And then the surprise. From two yards away, I hear the tone of Colonnese's voice change. He asks, 'Who says Venice is dead? It's time to stop lamenting. Rise up! Rise up! Do something! Yes, you too! ... And *stop saying that Venice is dead!*'

The caped organisers jump on the coffin and joyfully smash it to bits. From the splinters, they pull out a painting of a golden phoenix rising from the ashes. 'Long live Venice!' they cry.

This is not a funeral. It is an exorcism.

The death of Venice is pronounced dead. Venice is reborn. Everyone in the crowd cries, including me. The organisers shake the prosecco bottles and spray the press liberally with foam. Perhaps they already know what kind of wordbites will betray their intentions to the world. Who among these reporters will transmit the fact that this funeral has been staged by Venetians who refuse to let the city die?

Michelle Lovric, 'The Death of Venice is Dead' (2009)
A longer version of this piece was first posted on An Awfully Big
Blog Adventure (http://awfullybigblogadventure.blogspot.org) on
November 22nd, 2009.

❊ ❊ ❊

The last word, from D. H. Lawrence's Lady Chatterley's Lover, *sums up the almost overwhelming wealth of pleasure and entertainment to be found in one of the world's most extraordinary cities.*

Their father took them to the exhibition, miles and miles of weary paintings. He took them to all the cronies of his in the Villa Lucchese, he sat with them on warm evenings in the piazza, having got a table at Florian's: he took them to the theatre, to the Goldoni plays. There were illuminated water-fêtes, there were dances. This was a holiday-place of all holiday-places. The Lido, with its acres of sun-pinked or pyjamaed bodies, was like a strand with an endless head of seals come up for mating. Too many people in the piazza, too many limbs and trunks of humanity on the Lido, too many gondolas, too many motor-launches, too many steamers, too many pigeons, too many ices, too many cocktails, too many men-servants wanting tips, too many languages rattling, too much, too much sun, too much smell of Venice, too many cargoes of strawberries, too many silk shawls, too many huge, raw-beef slices of water-melon on stalls: too much enjoyment, altogether far too much enjoyment! [...]

It was *almost* enjoyment. But anyhow, with all the cocktails, all the lying in warmish water and sun-bathing on hot sand in hot sun, jazzing with your stomach up against some fellow in the warm nights, cooling off with ices, it was a complete narcotic. And that was what they all wanted, a drug: the slow water, a drug; the sun, a drug; jazz, a drug; cigarettes, cocktails, ices, vermouth. To be drugged! Enjoyment! Enjoyment!

D. H. Lawrence, *Lady Chatterley's Lover* (1928)

Parting (snap) shots

As we sail away over the Adriatic, or climb from the runway, or hurry to catch the train or coach, or pack the last souvenir into the car, each visitor takes away memories that are personal and particular, but also part of the collective experience of Venice. So, a few little snap-shots to jog the memory.

At sunset all cities look wonderful, but some more so than others. Reliefs become suppler, columns more rotund, capitals curlier, cornices more resolute, spires starker, niches deeper, disciples more draped, angels airborne. In the streets it gets dark, but it is still daytime for the Fondamenta and that gigantic liquid mirror where motorboats, vaporetti, gondolas, dinghies, and barges "like scattered old shoes" zealously trample baroque and Gothic façades, not sparing your own or a passing cloud's reflection either.

Joseph Brodsky, *Watermark* (1992)

✳ ✳ ✳

In the balmy noisy Venetian night with myriads of lights, illuminated domes and bridges, Pippa slipped through the *pensione* gates to wait by the stone lions where she could see the traffic of boats on the Grand Canal. As she stood there, she heard music, and a flotilla of gondolas passed slowly, the black hulls so close they seemed tied together and, in one, a singer stood under a light singing to an accordion player ...

Rumer Godden, *Pippa Passes* (1999)

✳ ✳ ✳

A bridge. A shadow. A masque we can't afford.

Vanessa Lyons, 'Whose Venice?' (2008)

✳ ✳ ✳

The boat slid under the elaborate iron footbridge connecting the island of San Pietro to the Arsenale. These were the hinder parts of the city, a dense mass of brick tenements formerly inhabited by the army of manual labourers employed in the dockyards. Nowhere were there more dead ends and fewer through routes, nowhere were the houses darker and more crowded, nowhere was the dialect thicker and more impenetrable.

Michael Dibdin, *Dead Lagoon* (1994)

✳ ✳ ✳

At the east end of the thronged square the Basilica of Saint Mark loomed out of the grey fog like a dream of oriental splendour. In the mist the brilliant colours of the mosaics and the marble columns seemed a little washed out, as though every tourist snapshot had stolen here a blush of rose, there a glitter of gold. On the balustrade above the central portal the bronze horses pawed the mist, two with the left foot, two with the right.

Jane Langton, *The Thief of Venice* (1999)

✳ ✳ ✳

A narrow canal in the heart of the city – a patch of green water and a surface of pink wall. [...] A girl crosses the little bridge, which has an arch like a camel's back.

Henry James, *Italian Hours* (1909)

✳ ✳ ✳

Coming out of the dim, leather-smelling cave of the handbag shop into the unique dazzle of a Venetian afternoon. Yes, it's the light, the light and ... so much else. But the light above all. I don't think even Canaletto got it right. Not quite.

Simona Luff, *Diary* (2006)

✳ ✳ ✳

On the other side of this small water-way is a great shabby façade of Gothic windows and balconies – balconies on which dirty clothes are hung and under which a cavernous-looking doorway opens from a low flight of slimy water-steps.

Henry James, *Italian Hours* (1909)

✳ ✳ ✳

Piazza San Marco, so lovely in photographs or at dawn, so pigeon-congested once the day got going.

Geoff Dyer, *Jeff in Venice* (2009)

✳ ✳ ✳

Venice – strawberry ice-cream and a box of trinkets?

Vanessa Lyons, 'Whose Venice?' (2008)

Selective Index

Names marked with * indicate writers whose work is extracted in this volume.

Acknowledgements

Oxygen Books would like to thank all those who have helped in the preparation of this volume, particularly Jeff Cotton, Michelle Lovric, Eduardo Reyes, Wendy Sanford, and Catherine Trippett.

Barbaro, Paolo, *Venice Revealed* Copyright © 1998 Marsilio Editions. English language edition (translated by Tami Calliope) copyright © 2001 Steerforth Press. Reprinted by permission of Souvenir Books.

Berendt, John, *City of Falling Angels* Copyright © John Berendt 2005. Reproduced by permission of Hodder and Stoughton Limited.

Bhabra, H. S., *Gestures* Published by Michael Joseph, 1986; Penguin Books, 1987. Copyright © The Estate of 6. Reproduced with permission of Johnson and Alcock Ltd.

Bidisha, *Venetian Masters* Copyright © Bidisha, 2008. Reproduced with permission of Summersdale Publishers Ltd.

Brodsky, Joseph, *Watermark* Copyright © 1992 by Joseph Brodsky. Published by The Noonday Press, New York. Reprinted by permission of Farrar, Straus and Giroux.

Brophy, Brigid, *The King of a Rainy Country* Copyright © Brigid Brophy 1956. First published by Martin Secker and Warburg Ltd, 1956; published by Virago Press Limited, 1990. Reproduced by permission of Sheil Land Associates Ltd. on behalf of the Estate of Brigid Brophy.

Casanova, Giacomo, *The Story of my Life* English translation copyright © Stephen Sarterelli and Sophie Hawkes, 2000. Published by Penguin Books, 2001.

de Beauvoir, Simone, *Force of Circumstance* Copyright © 1963 The Estate of Simone de Beauvoir, and Éditions Gallimard, Paris. Reproduced by kind permission of the Estate of Simone de Beauvoir, and Éditions Gallimard, Paris, c/o Rosica Colin Limited, London.

Demski, Eva, *Venedig. Salon der Welt* © Schöffling & Co. Verlagsbuchhandlung GmbH, Frankfurt am Main 1996. Translation Susan Thorne 2010.

de Prada, Juan Manuel, *The Tempest* Copyright © Juan Manuel de Prada 1997. Reproduced by permission of Hodder and Stoughton Limited.

Dibdin, Michael, *Dead Lagoon* Copyright © Michael Dibdin, 1994. Reprinted by permission of Faber and Faber Ltd.

du Maurier, Daphne, *Don't Look Now* Copyright © Daphne du Maurier, 1971. First published by Victor Gollanz 1971; Penguin edition, 1973; Penguin Classics edition, 2006. Reproduced by permission of Curtis Brown Group Ltd on behalf of The Chichester Partnership.

Dyer, Geoff, *Jeff in Venice, Death in Varanasi* Copyright © Geoff Dyer, 2009. Reprinted by permission of Canongate Books Ltd, Edinburgh.

Godden, Rumer, *Pippa Passes* Copyright © Rumer Godden 1994. Published by Macmillan London, 1994; Pan Books edition, 1995. Reprinted by permission of the Curtis Brown Group Ltd. London on behalf of The Estate of Rumer Godden.

Goethe, Johann Wolfgang von, *Italian Journey* Translated by W. H. Auden and Elizabeth Mayer. Published by Penguin Classics, 1970. Copyright © 1962, 1970, The Estate of W. H. Auden. Reprinted by permission of The Wylie Agency on behalf of the Estate of W. H. Auden.

Hartley, L. P., *Eustace and Hilda* Copyright © L. P. Hartley, 1947. Reprinted by permission of Faber and Faber Ltd.

Highsmith, Patricia, *The Talented Mr Ripley* Copyright © Patricia Highsmith 1955,1956. Copyright © renewed by Patricia Highsmith 1983. Reprinted by permission of the Random House Group Ltd.

Hill, Susan, *The Man in the Picture* Copyright © Susan Hill, 2007. Reprinted by permission of Profile Books Ltd.

Hopkinson, Amanda, 'A Student in Venice'. Published by permission of the author.

Ishiguro, Kazuo, *Nocturnes* Copyright © Kazuo Ishiguro, 2009. Reproduced by permission of the author c/o Rogers Coleridge and White Ltd., 20 Powis Mews, London W11 1JN.

Kanon, Joseph, *Alibi* Copyright © 2005 by Joseph Kanon. Published by Henry Holt and Company under license from Pan Books. Reprinted with permission of St Martin's Press, part of the Macmillan Group, USA.

Langton, Jane, *The Thief of Venice* Copyright © Jane Langton 1999. Published by Penguin USA. Reprinted with permission of Penguin USA.

Leon, Donna, *Death at La Fenice* Copyright © Donna Leon 1992. Published by Chapman Brothers, 1992; Arrow Books 2004; reissued by Arrow Books 2009. Reprinted by permission of the Random House Group Ltd.

Leon, Donna, *The Anonymous Venetian* Copyright © Donna Leon 1994. Published by Macmillan 1994. Pan Books edition 1995. Reprinted by permission of Pan Macmillan.

Lively, Penelope, *Perfect Happiness* Copyright © Penelope Lively, 1983. First published by William Heinemann Ltd 1983; Penguin edition 1985. Reprinted by kind permission of David Higham Associates.

Lovric, M. R., *Carnevale* Copyright © M. R. Lovric 2001. Published by Virago Press 2001. Reprinted by permission of the Little, Brown Group Ltd.

Lovric, M. R., *The Floating Book* Copyright © Michelle Lovric 2003. Published by Virago Press 2003. Reprinted by permission of the Little Brown Group Ltd.

Lovric, Michelle, 'Emilio's Legs' Copyright © Michelle Lovric 2010. Reprinted by permission of the author.

Lovric, Michelle, 'The Death of Venice is Dead' Copyright © Michelle Lovric 2010. Reprinted by permission of the author.

Lovric, Michelle, 'Waterproofing' Copyright © Michelle Lovric 2009. www.englishwritersinitaly.com , November 2009. Reprinted by permission of the author.

Luff, Simona, *Diary* Copyright © Simona Luff 2006. Reprinted by permission of the author.

Lyons, Vanessa, 'Whose Venice?' (from 'Travels with a Notebook') Copyright © Vanessa Lyons 2010. Reprinted by kind permission of the author.

MacCaulay, Kay, *The Man Who Was Loved* Copyright Kay MacCauley. Reprinted by kind permission of Saqi Books.

Mann, Thomas, *Death in Venice*, translated by H. T. Lowe-Porter. First published in German in 1912. Published in great Britain by Martin Secker and Warburg Ltd, 1928; Penguin edition 1955. Reprinted by permission of the Random House Group Ltd.

Martin, Judith, *No Vulgar Hotel* Copyright © 2007 by Judith Martin. Reprinted by permission of W. W. Norton & Company Ltd, New York.

Matvejević, Predrag, *The Other Venice*, first published in English by Reaktion Books, London, 2007. English language translation © Reaktion Books, 2007. English language translation by Russell Scott Valentino. This book is a revised edition of *L'Autre Venise* by Predrag Matvejević © Librairie Arthème Fayard, 2004.

McCarthy, Mary, *Venice Observed* copyright © Mary McCarthy, 1963. Reprinted by kind permission of A. M. Heath and Co. Ltd.

McEwan, Ian, *The Comfort of Strangers* Copyright © 1981 Ian McEwan. Reproduced by permission of the author c/o Rogers, Coleridge & White Ltd., 20 Powis Mews, London W11.

Morris, Jan, *Europe: An Intimate Journey* Copyright © Jan Morris, 1997, 2006. Reprinted by permission of Faber and Faber Ltd.

Morris, Jan, *Venice* Copyright © James Morris, 1960; © Jan Morris, 1974, 1983. Reprinted by permission of Faber and Faber Ltd.

Philips, Caryl, *The Nature of Blood* Copyright © Caryl Phillips, 1997. First published by Faber and Faver Ltd 1997. Published by Vintage

2008. Reprinted by permission of The Random House Group Ltd.

Proust, Marcel, *The Fugitive* First published 1925. English translation by C. K. Scott Moncrieff and Terence Kilmartin, revised by D. J. Enright. Translation copyright © Chatto and Windus and Random House Inc. 1981. Copyright in revision to translation © D. J. Enright 1992. reprinted by permission of The Random House Group Ltd.

Purves, Libby, *More Lives Than One* Copyright © 1998 Libby Purves. First published in 1998 by Hodder and Stoughton (Sceptre). Reprinted by permission of Hodder and Stoughton Ltd.

Scarpa, Tiziano, *Venice is a Fish* Copyright © 2000 Giangiacomo Feltrinelli Editore Milano. Translation copyright © 2008 Shaun Whiteside. Translation first published in 2008 by Serpent's Tail, an imprint of Profile Books Ltd.. Reprinted by permission of Profile Books Ltd.

Seth, Vikram, *An Equal Music* Copyright Vikram Seth 1999. First published in 1999 by Phoenix House. Reprinted by permission of The Orion Publishing Group Ltd.

Unsworth, Barry, *Stone Virgin* Copyright © Barry Unsworth, 1985. First published by Hamish Hamilton 1985. Penguin edition 1986. Reprinted by permission of Penguin Books and the Sheil Land Associates Ltd on behalf of the author.

Vickers, Sally, *Miss Garnet's Angel* Copyright © Sally Vickers 2000. First published by Fourth Estate 2000. Harper Perennial Edition 2007. Reprinted by permission of HarperCollins Publishers Ltd.

Waugh, Evelyn, *Brideshead Revisited* Copyright © 1945 by Evelyn Waugh. Copyright renewed © 1972, 1973 by Mrs Laura Waugh. First published by Chapman & Hall, 1945. Reprinted by permission of The Wylie Agency and The Estate of Evelyn Waugh.

Winterson, Jeanette, *The Passion* Copyright © Jeanette Winterson 1987. First published by Bloomsbury 1987. Penguin edition 1988. Published by kind permission of the PFD Agency on behalf of the author.

Every effort has been made to trace and contact copyright holders before publication. If notified, the publisher will rectify any errors or omissions at the earliest opportunity.

217

An exciting and unique travel series featuring the best-ever writing on European and World cities

Praise for *city-lit PARIS*

'An essential guidebook ... It maps the Paris of the imagination beautifully'

Kate Muir, author of *Left Bank*

'It's terrific ... all the best writing on this complex city in one place'

Professor Andrew Hussey, author of *Paris: The Secret History*

'A great and eclectic set of writings ... an original book on Paris'

Sylvia Whitman, Shakespeare & Co, Paris

'It's like having your own iPad loaded with different tomes, except that this slim anthology contains only the best passages, bite-sized chunks just perfect to dip into as you sip that pastis in a pavement café.'

The Times

'Whether you're a newcomer to Paris or a die-hard aficionado, this gem of a book will make you think of the city in a completely new way'

Living France

'The ideal book for people who don't want to leave their minds at the airport'

Celia Brayfield, author of *Deep France*

'The *city-lit PARIS* guide is essential reading for anyone remotely interested in Paris, or planning a visit'

Mike Gerrard, best-selling travel guide writer

'This innovative guide takes us from Marcel Proust on that perfect erotic moment to Gertrude Stein on the origins of the croissant to Agnès Catherine Poirier on the lure of the Paris café'

Paris Voice

'Go to any bookshop and the shelf labelled 'Paris' is always packed with tomes about the French capital. But the first in a new series of travel guides holds more intrigue than most – because it contains the musings of some seriously big-name writers ... We think it's just ideal for those Paris lovers fond of a finely crafted phrase.'

French Magazine

'Features work from Kate Mosse, Julian Barnes, Marcel Proust, Irène Némirovsky and Stephen Clarke - over seventy writers in all. It is a really neat idea with some amazing writers included.'

Scott Pack, *Me and My Big Mouth*

'This compilation of short stories and writings sheds new light on the city, covering topics ranging from café culture through to famous Parisians and

Praise for city-lit PARIS

their daily activities (ever wanted to know exactly how much absinthe Verlaine could drink in one session?) ...Whether you're a newcomer to Paris or a die-hard aficionado, this gem of a book will make you think of the city in a completely new way.'

France

'When is a travel guide not a travel guide? When it's a City-lit guide - supremely readable and full of wonderful holiday ideas for your next city break in Paris or London ...Get a unique feel for the sights, sounds and flavours of the city that only the very best writers can provide.'

travelbite.co.uk

£8.99 ISBN 978–0–9559700–0–9

Praise for *city-lit LONDON*

'This treasure trove of a book ... a unique way to explore the ever-changing landscape of a city, through the voices of those that know it intimately'
Rachel Lichtenstein, author of *On Brick Lane*

'For those visitors to London who seek to do more than bag Big Ben and Buckingham Palace, this is the ideal guide, a collection of writings that expose not only the city's secret places but its very soul ... I can't imagine a more perfect travelling companion than this wonderful anthology'
Clare Clark, author of *The Great Stink*

'Brings London to life past and present in a way no conventional guide book could ever achieve'
Tarquin Hall, author of *Salaam Brick Lane*

'The latest offering in this impressive little series concentrates on the spirit of London as seen through the eyes of an eclectic selection of writers. Part of the joy of this collection is that the writers span several centuries, which means that multiple faces of London are revealed. It's an exciting selection, with unexpected gems from novelists, travel writers, journalists and bloggers. Keith Waterhouse, for example, writes with gentle pathos about the double life of a transvestite in Soho; Vita Sackville-West wryly observes a coronation in Westminster Abbey; Virginia Woolf promenades down Oxford Street; and Dostoyevsky strolls down the Haymarket'
Clover Stroud, *The Sunday Telegraph*

'For some time now, small publisher Oxygen has been producing the excellent city-lit series, which uses descriptions of a city penned by writers, both living and dead to illuminate the metropolis in question. The most recent is London, compiled by Heather Reyes. This includes Jan Morris arriving at Heathrow, Monica Ali on Brick Lane, Virginia Woolf shopping in Oxford Street, Barbara Cartland at a West End Ball, Dostoyevsky strolling down Haymarket and Will Self inside the head of a cab driver'
Giles Foden, *Condé Nast Traveller*

'We can't declare it with absolute certainty, but it's a fair bet that Dame Barbara Cartland and Diamond Geezer have never before snuggled up between the same covers. *City-lit: LONDON* places these strange bedfellows alongside Will Self, Virginia Woolf, Alan Bennett and sixty others in a frenzied orgy of London writing. You'll love it'
Londonist

'The second volume in this enticing new series includes extracts from the work of 60 wonderfully diverse writers, including Will Self, Monica Ali, Alan Bennett, Dostoyevsky, and yes, Barbara Cartland (writing about a West End ball)'
Editor's Pick, *The Bookseller*

£8.99 ISBN: 978–0–9559700–5–4

Praise for *city-lit BERLIN*

'A gem ... an elegant, enjoyable and essential book'

Rosie Goldsmith, BBC Radio 4

'This wonderful anthology explores what it is really like to be a Berliner by bringing together extracts about the city from a range of genres, including some specially translated. This was the city of Einstein, Brecht, George Grosz, and Marlene Dietrich. It was 'the New York of the old world', a melting pot of new ideas and lifestyles ... This collection is timely: on 9 November 20 years ago, Berliners tore down the hated wall'

The Guardian

'*city-Lit Berlin* gathers more than a hundred extracts from writers on aspects of Berlin's conflicted heritage ... the editors have trawled widely to try to capture the modern city's rule-bound yet permissive tone, as well as its persistent state of cultural and architectural renewal. The result is an eclectic pillow-book ... a stimulating intellectual tour of the idea of the city that would complement any guidebook's more practical orientation'

Financial Times

'This is a sublime introduction to the city'

Sydney Morning Herald

'A fascinating cornucopia of Berlin writing by authors such as John Simpson, Ian McEwan and Anna Funder; artists such as David Bowie and Marlene Dietrich, and writers such as Jeffrey Eugenides, Philip Kerr and Thomas Pynchon. The beauty of this clever series is the breadth and reach of its contributors, be they artists, musicians, musos or writers – in turn, each lays claim to the city.

Many were inspired by the Wall coming down, the inventive vibe, or simply the cheap rents – all took ease in the bohemian exuberance the city offered up. This collection of writing gives a flavour to a city that has long nurtured its artists, giving them space to create, whether for one week or a lifetime'

Caroline Eden, *Real Travel Magazine*

'Although there are plenty of old favourites such as Christopher Isherwood, Alfred Döblin and Len Deighton, the emphasis of the book is on unexpected vantage points and new, less familiar voices. So there is no dutiful trot through the city's history "from earliest times to the present day", but instead themed sections which try to get under the skin of the city.'

George Miller, Podularity

'Another in this sterling series of city-writing compilations, this one follows the pattern of short excerpts gathered into chapters, that this time vary from the arbitrarily-themed to the perfect. The simplest one is also the most gripping: it's called 'The past is another country', but don't let that put you off. Its well-chosen pieces take you through Berlin's history from the early 19th Century to today, and make for an almost perfect, and very moving, slice through history. (It's interesting to note that even in the 1920s Berlin was a place renowned for building over its history.) The book choices are as eclectic as you could wish for, taking in most of the authors listed above – including the obvious choices like Isherwood, Kerr, Le Carré and Deighton – and some stuff new to me. Top of the list of latter includes Ian Walker's *Zoo Station* and Beatrice Colin's *The Luminous Life of Lilly Aphrodite*. Further interest is added by co-editor Katy Derbyshire's translations of bits from works not otherwise available in English. This manages to be not just a fine and fascinating introduction to the literature, but to rise above its expected status as a dipping thing to become a mighty fine cover-to-cover read in itself'

Jeff Cotton, *Fictional Cities*

'A welcome contrast to the many formulaic travel guides in print and online, *city-Lit Berlin* reveals the city as seen through the eyes of 60 writers of all description – from novelists such as Christopher Isherwood and Ian McEwan to local bloggers like Simon Cole, reporters (Kate Adie), historians (Peter Gay) and untranslated German writers, including Inka Parei, whose novel *Die Scha-teenboxerin* (The Shadow-Boxing Woman) captures the volatility of Berlin in the Nineties, just a few years after the Wall collapsed. We keep David Bowie company as he cycles around the city, and contemplate Marlene Dietrich's grave in a volume that has greatly enriched the field of travel books.'

Ralph Fields, *Nash Magazine*

£8.99 ISBN 978–0–9559700–4–7

Praise for *city-pick DUBLIN*

'For a population that barely reaches one million, Dublin has produced a staggering four Nobel prize winners. This new addition to the city-pick series is a reminder of Dublin's rich literary history, as well as an introduction to its contemporary forms. Drinking, music and rebellion loom large in these short pieces from Irish legends of letters such as Brendan Behan, Samuel Beckett and Sean O'Casey, which sit comfortably alongside extracts from modern writers such as Roddy Doyle and Colm Toibin. Cumulatively they build an elegant, incisive and always entertaining guide to the city's multitude of literary lives.'

Lonely Planet Magazine

'*city-pick Dublin* is the latest triumph of distillation. There's everything here from David Norris' defence of the significance of Joyce's *Ulysses* to Iris Murdoch's fictional treatment of The Easter Rising. You'll read about walking and drinking, being poor and being poetic, new wealth and newcomers, old timers and returning natives. In her introduction to *city-pick Dublin*, Orna Ross says that going by "great writers per head of population" Dublin is "the clear winner" in any "survey of literary destinations." As this is the city of Wilde, Shaw, Yeats, Beckett, Heaney, Swift *et* many a brilliant *al*, how could anyone disagree?'

Garan Holcombe, Book of the Month, *The Good Web Guide*

'A book you can't miss'

The Lady

'Vastly different from the usual travel guide, the city pick series offers first hand writing from a city's brightest wordsmiths and the Dublin edition brings the best out of its home grown talent. With over one hundred extracts from over sixty different writers including Roddy Doyle, Samuel Beckett and Chris Binchy there will be plenty of inspiration for exploring the famous streets of the Irish capital.'

Travelbite

'A UNIQUE travel guide, published this week, is planning to show a different side to Dublin by bringing to life its rich and diverse history of literature. city-pick Dublin, published by Oxygen Books, has brought together 50 writers and more than 100 extracts to bring famous Dubliners to life. Respected author and journalist Orna Ross, who writes the foreword, describes Dublin as one of the most literary rich cities in the world ... The timing for this book couldn't be better as Dublin celebrates becoming a UNESCO World City of Literature in 2010, which will showcase the diverse and experimental talent from this small city.'

The Irish Post

'The next in this excellent *city-pick* series, with some 100 plus extracts from a diverse collection of writers ... more than 50 of the very best writers on Dublin

Praise for city-pick DUBLIN

including William Trevor, Flann O'Brien, Joseph O'Connor, Brendan Behan, Anne Enright, Roddy Doyle and Maeve Binchy.

The Bookseller

'From Sean O'Casey to Anne Enright – the best ever writing on Dublin has been specially published in a new book entitled *city-pick Dublin*'

RTÉ

'Bite-sized beauties ... You won't find pub recommendations or directions to art galleries in this little guide, but you will get a taste of Dublin's most important natural resource: stories.'

The Dubliner

£8.99 ISBN 978–0–9559700–1–6

Praise for *city-pick* AMSTERDAM

'This latest addition to the excellent 'city-pick' series of urban anthologies weaves together fiction and non-fiction, including more than 30 specially translated extracts, to give an intimate portrait of one of Europe's most distinctive cities.'

The Guardian

'This engrossing book ... Some of the names in *city-pick Amsterdam* – such as the historian Simon Schama – may be familiar to British readers, but there are plenty more contributions in translation from Dutch writers.'

Lonely Planet Magazine

'Charles de Montesquieu, David Sedaris and Cees Nooteboom walk into a bruin café. It's not the start of a bad bibiliophile joke, but the portrait painted by a new breed of city guide ... It's a simple idea, presenting a metropolis in all its multifaceted glory through the words of great writers; and it's one so good it's astonishing it hasn't been done before. Split into loosely thematic sections, one of the nicest features of this collection are the 70-plus contributors – novelists, journalists, travel writers – span the centuries. There's a thoughtful selection of Dutch writers including not only literary heavyweights like Mak, who are widely known in translation, but also lesser-known authors – Meijsing, Stefan Hertmans, Jan Donkers – some of whom are translated into English for the first time. It makes for some delightful discoveries – even for those of us who think we know this city well'

Time Out Amsterdam

'The latest clever city-pick compendium of travel writing takes us to Amsterdam in some excellent company. Like other books in this unique series, it brings together more than a hundred extracts culled from other works, providing a one-stop reference for Amsterdam, that great city of trade, sin and exiles ... Essential – slip it into your bag, alongside a Rough Guide'

Waterstone's Books Quarterly

'The most recent addition to the Oxygen Books city-picks series is Amsterdam, edited by Heather Reyes (£8.99), which pulls together a decent clutch of extracts from interesting living writers – Ian McEwan, Geoff Dyer and Simon Schama – waxing incidentally, hedonistically and historically on the Dutch city of sin – as well as snippets from even grander dead scribes, including Smollett, Voltaire and Camus. It's a canny publishing idea, as Oxygen can show off a top-notch set of writers through short extracts.'

Time Out London

'The *city-pick* guide to Amsterdam definitely didn't disappoint – with plenty of short excerpts from longer works, I found it to be fantastic option for reading during my morning commute, as I could dip in and out of it easily, momentarily escaping mentally from the daily grind. But I could also imagine it to be an excellent choice for a traveller who is about to board a plane or train to Amsterdam – no one piece requires too much attention, making it a fabulous travelling companion ... By the time I finished reading this book, I felt like I had a great understanding for not just the sights of Amsterdam that every visitor should see, but also for the history and people that make the city unique.'

Travelbite

'The latest instalment in this much-lauded series, *city-pick: Amsterdam* show-cases all the qualities that have established *city-pick* as an innovative literary alternative to your average visitor's potted history or guidebook. Eclectic, challenging and deeply involved in its subject, it takes you to deeper, more diverse places than you could ever hope to go elsewhere.'

Translated Fiction

£8.99 ISBN 978–0–9559700–2–3

www.oxygenbooks.co.uk